AF241867

Pure Contradiction

RAINER MARIA RILKE

Pure Contradiction

Selected Poems

Translated and introduced by
Ian Crockatt

2012

Published by Arc Publications,
Nanholme Mill, Shaw Wood Road
Todmorden OL14 6DA, UK

Design by Tony Ward
Printed by Lightning Source

978 1906570 22 4 (pbk)
978 1906570 44 6 (hbk)

The translator gratefully acknowledges the award of a writer's bursary by Scottish Arts Council to enable the completion of this project, and the permission granted by Insel Verlag, Frankfurt am Main, for the use of the German texts.

Cover painting by Wenna Crockatt

The publishers acknowledge financial assistance from ACE Yorkshire

'Arc Classics:
NewTranslations of Great Poets of the Past'
Series Editor: Jean Boase-Beier

Acknowledgements

In making these translations, I have freely consulted other translators' work, particularly that of Stephen Mitchell, Edward Snow and Stuart Cohn; but also including J. B. Leishman, C. F. McIntyre, Michael Hamburger, David Oswald, Don Paterson, Jo Shapcott and A. Poulin, Jr. My thanks to them all.

At the same time I have tried to bear in mind Gerald Manley Hopkins' practice regarding other peoples' work: "admire, and do otherwise".

Some of these translations were published first in *Northwords Now*.

Thank you to Stuart B. Campbell and Philip Wilson who read the translations in manuscript and commented constructively and in detail on the many shortcomings they found – those that remain are solely mine.

Thanks also to Jean Boase-Beier and George Szirtes respectively for their encouragement; to my brother Richard who started all this by introducing me to Rilke and who has generously supported me throughout; and special thanks and love to Wenna who weathered the "Rilke years" with a tolerance I hardly deserved.

Ian Crockatt

CONTENTS

INTRODUCTION

During his lifetime Rainer Maria Rilke was revered by poetry lovers throughout Europe. The Russian poet Marina Tsvetaeva's remark in a letter to him that he is "not a poet, but the very embodiment of poetry" captures the feeling. It seems that it still prevails, particularly amongst poets, if the continual stream of English language translations and commentaries by them is anything to go by – I have a dozen from the last sixty years or so next to me now, and there are more, as well as a generous scattering of single poem translations amongst other poets' collections of their own work. Of course Rilke wrote so much poetry, and so much about his life, that it is unlikely that most of us have read all of it. Most have translated selections from his books, or have focused on particular ones – *Duino Elegies*, *Sonnets to Orpheus*, *New Poems*, *The Book of Hours*, *The Book of Images*, poems not published by Rilke in his lifetime, and his French language poems being the main groups.

So why another? It's not a question generally asked of the director of a new production of Hamlet, or the producer of a new CD of Beethoven's ninth symphony – we accept that there is an infinity of interpretations possible of the most profound works of art; that is part of their greatness. In fact we constantly seek new approaches and insights which will further our understanding and appreciation of them, and so, we believe, of our own elusive natures. Much of Rilke's work achieves this exalted level of mastery and appeal – many, for example, refer to the *Duino Elegies* as the highest achievement of twentieth-century poetry in any European language.

The purpose of this small selection is to add a particularity of approach to the corpus of Rilke translation and, by so doing, to illuminate the richness of language, thought and feeling it communicates from an infrequently explored angle. The focus is on interconnectedness, the sense that the poetry, letters and prose Rilke produced in such enormous profusion throughout his life, are developments – variations, diversifications, departures – of and from the idiosyncratic set of ideas and themes he arrived at when he was a very young man. This is best illustrated by the discussion developed later in this introduction about the order in which the poems are arranged in this volume, and examples of how some, though written twenty or more years apart, can gain from relation with each other.

One idea in particular which Rilke frequently expresses in words, but which he also physically and emotionally lived, is that there is a basic conflict between life, in its bourgeois forms in Europe, and the work of a purely dedicated artist – to be the one he had to sacrifice the other. Even in a post-modern age which would rather take the text for what it is than approach it as a product of its writer, this makes Rilke's biography of unusual significance to his art. I therefore think that before discussing the arrangement of the poems in this selection, and the reasons for it, a brief overview of the external features of his life, and some links between it and his writing, will be helpful.

Rilke – christened René Karl Wilhelm Johann Josef Maria – was born in Prague in 1875, a time when Prague was part of the Austrian empire. Rilke's family was part of the minority but dominant German-speaking elite, contemptuous of their Czech neighbours, but neither rich nor high in status. His father was invalided out of the army before achieving his ambition of gaining a commission, and lived a life of disappointment working for the railways. His abiding hope was that his only son would gain distinction in the army instead. The family had notions of being descended from an aristocratic strain of Rilkes, and René never lost the air and pretensions implicit in this (mistaken) belief. The force in his family was his mother, who was religious, sentimental and theatrical, and had snobbish ambitions for her son. Her apparent disappointment that he was not a girl – an older sister had died in infancy – plus his delicacy, resulted in him being brought up as one for his first five years; and yet, his parents having separated when he was 9 years old, he was bundled off to a military school by his father when aged just 11. Rilke frequently refers to his five years of suffering there – he was finally allowed to leave on account of his poor health.

But by this time he was already writing, both poetry and prose, as well as involved in the production of plays and other literary projects. Between 1892 and 1896 he seems to have been an embarrassingly eager, over-prolific, fay and frequently derivative writer, a character in Prague literary circles who could sometimes be seen walking the streets in contemplation of an iris held in front of him. Nevertheless his work, in particular his poetry's brand of quasi-religious heightened sensibility and its technical virtuosity, attracted attention – by the age of 21 he had already published three books of poetry, as well as stories and novellas.

From these beginnings an immensely individual and uncompromising writer emerged, one who committed himself so completely to his art that serving it, making himself available to its demands, creating the optimum con-ditions for uninterrupted response when real inspiration arrived, took priority over commitment to relationships and sustained human intercourse. His marriage in 1901 to Clara Westhoff, a sculptor pupil of Rodin and mem-ber of an artist's colony in Worspede, Germany, lasted a lifetime in the sense of continuing contact, but only a few months of actually living together. Rilke had to sac-rifice the conventional benefits and comforts of living a domestic life with his wife and daughter, to the nomadic, emotionally and sexually uncommitted life of the committed artist. As his work increasingly made him famous his many liaisons with women – some rich and generous patrons – his wanderings between their houses, hotel rooms and briefly rented flats throughout Europe – punctuated by begging letters to his ever-indulgent publisher as well as production of his increasingly successful books – allowed an outwardly shapeless and yet utterly purposeful life dedicated to his art to develop.

Paris, where he based himself in his earlier days, was of particular importance to Rilke, and it was a city he both feared and loved. His only novel, *The Notebooks of Malte Laurids Brigge*, painfully written over a period of six years, gives an extraordinary, hallucinatory account of the near breakdown of a sensitive psyche in the face of the heartbreak and grotesquery of its street-life. He made two trips to Russia with Lou Andreas-Salomé, the fascinatingly intelligent and beautiful woman who was one of the first of her gender in Europe to attend university, was wooed unsuccessfully for three years by Nietzsche, and who, in later life, became a friend of Freud and one of the first psychoanalysts. It was Lou – for a while Rilke's lover – who was responsible for Rilke changing his name from René to Rainer. She, and through her Russia, remained important to him throughout his life. So too did Rodin, the sculptor he regarded as Europe's foremost artist and to whom he was secretary for two years. Through observing Rodin's single-minded absorption in his work, and the ferocity of his concentration whether or not he felt 'inspired', Rilke developed a new focus and physicality in his writing. This new engagement with Things, the attempt to internalise the inner essence of objects and re-express them through the subtly tuned medium of his inwardly focused poetry, is most clearly demonstrated in the 180 or so poems which make up the two volumes of *New Poems*, published in 1906 and 1908.

Rilke's ability to change his work in response to the influences and circumstances currently at play is not, however, either instant or superficial. Once he had written 'Panther', his famous first New Poem after following, it is said, Rodin's advice to go to the zoo and observe, he continued to produce poems in his earlier style. It was a further two years before he set to work to develop this new approach which so fundamentally underscores his later work, as well as sounding a substantially new note in European poetry. Later, in 1912, while staying alone at Duino Castle on the Adriatic sea – it belonged to his supporter and patron Princess Maria von Thurn und Taxis-Hohenlohe – he 'received' the first lines and overall scheme of what he knew was to become his great work, lines redolent with a sonorous intensity and expansiveness of understanding and purpose new to him and yet, all his life, anticipated. Nevertheless it was another ten years before he was able to find the physical place, the undisturbed time and the repose of mind which were the conditions he knew he required to finally complete – in an overwhelming few days which he described as 'a hurricane of the spirit' – not just the ten *Duino Elegies*, but also the entirely different, unexpected, series of fifty five exquisite *Sonnets to Orpheus*. This conscious, apparently pre-destined element in Rilke's understanding of his task as a poet, the years of disappointed suffering when he could write little he valued – after initial euphoria he was spiritually devastated by the first world war – is characteristic. There is a sense in which he sees himself as a vessel waiting to be filled, is willing it, but knows that the moment cannot be forced – it will arrive when he has enabled the most propitious conditions for its development. Seen next to his frustrated longing for an idealised woman as life-long partner, this sense of reaching towards a difficult-to-arrive-at state has a reality and depth which makes it, as much as the knowledge of his apartness from others, the true root of the yearning which so strongly flavours his poetry. For Rilke, consummation means the fulfilment of his potential as an artist, which in itself he seems to have regarded as an elevation of the fully realised, all-encompassing artist to god-like status. Rilke was 57 years old when the Elegies and Sonnets arrived. His description of himself pacing a small room in the Château de Muzot – a small semi-fortified tower in Switzerland which he was first lent and then gifted by another admirer and patron – gives a graphic picture of how he experienced this high-point of his existence. He describes himself spending days and nights in his upstairs room, pacing back and forth, "howling unbelievably vast commands and receiving signals from cosmic space and booming out to them my immense salvos of welcome." He knew he had in some sense fulfilled his destiny, said it all. Nevertheless his last four years were immensely productive, both of a poetry which arguably reaches an even greater fluidity and penetration of the impenetrable than before, and a major body of work written in French – he felt that the German language could not express at that stage all he needed to say. With strong premonitions of his approaching death – a long and excruciating surrender to leukaemia – he threw himself into life, spending January to August of 1925 being fêted in the city of his first years away from home, Paris, and luxuriating in the agreeable attentions of young women. He died at Muzot in December 1926, his enigmatic epitaph already penned.

As noted, Rilke's preoccupations and themes were arrived at early, and constantly explored. He himself states in a letter to Lou Andreas-Salomé that the subject matter of his poems is only a pretext for working on underlying lifelong themes. These include the nature and significance of making 'song', death-in-life, the artist-God, the perniciousness of Christianity, the celebration of sex, the nature of women, love and loss, the natural earth, work versus life, isolation, the inwardness and connectedness of all Things, praise. His poetic building-blocks and symbols – Orpheus, angels, animals, trees and flowers, the heart, hands, dancers, mirrors, blood, sleep, mountains, wind, stars, the seasons, cries, distortions of time – are stitched into the ever-changing fabric of the poems he creates from these themes throughout the whole work. From an early stage Rilke manages the poet-alchemist's trick of combining concrete imagery with the most elusively expressed ideas, moving between the external and internal worlds convincingly and at will. Look at the movement in 'Early Apollo' from imagined lyrical roses sprouting from a stone statue's brow, to petals, through rain experienced as kisses on the trembling half-open mouth's lips, and back via the temptations of truth to pure song –

> and his brow is too young to have earned praise; though
> it's not too hard to conceive of lyrical roses, high-
>
> stemmed and perfumed, sprouting out of it, petal
> after petal loosed from his eyebrows falling
> as tender rain to his lips, subtle
>
> as kisses on his unawakened mouth,
> which trembles, half-smiling, as if new truths
> were tempting it with unbearably pure song.

(p. 25)

Or, from *Sonnets to Orpheus* Book 2 number 3, the interplay between abstraction, the figurative and the mystical –

15

> Here amongst the vanishing, in the realm of failure,
> be the sounding glass that shatters as it sounds. Be,…

(p. 103)

Or, from 'On the Verge of Night' – the literal and metaphorical distances travelled between micro and macro worlds, the personal and the universal.

> My room, and space watching
> over the land's dark distances –
> are one. I am a string
> stretched across the far-reaching
> thundering resonances.
>
> Things are violin-bodies
> full of reverberating darkness –
> in it dream the cries
> of women, in its sleep the bitterness
> of whole generations is roused…

(p. 83)

Always a technician of the highest calibre, these extracts also indicate the fluency with which Rilke could expand an idea outwards from the inner, the delicacy with which he could move between the sensual and the conceptual – he responded instinctively to the tensions latent in their juxtaposition. Undoubtedly his passionate study of Cézanne's paintings as well as of Rodin's sculptures made its contribution to this grounding of his elevated, spiritual inclinations in observed reality.

For some, of course, Rilke still remains too far out on the limb of self-regard and posturing – the poet John Berryman, for example, irritated by his preciousness, referred to him as 'a jerk'. Some of what he wrote in his letters is certainly either excruciatingly sensitive, or, to modern ears, grandly condescending – witness the first of Rilke's justly famous 'Letters to a Young Poet', towards the end of its portentous outpouring of advice –

> 'What more shall I say to you? Everything seems to me to
> have its proper emphasis. I would finally just like to ad-
> vise you to grow through your development quietly and
> seriously; you can interrupt it in no more violent manner
> than by looking outwards...' –

written when he was twenty seven to a twenty year old
would-be poet. Rilke's awareness of his own calling as a
poet, and his immersing of himself in the role to the extent
he did – as well, of course, as his controversial deliberations
on love, sex and religious observation – have resulted in
a guru-like status and following in some quarters. Few
have played the quirky, over-sensitive, other-worldly poet
to such effect – except that, as described above, in Rilke's
case it was never a game; he lived it.

*

The arrangement of the poems in this selection reflects
the proposition that there are poems from all stages of
Rilke's life which are thematically congruent, or share a
feeling or a similar imaginative starting point. By mak-
ing bedfellows of poems rarely seen side by side before
I hope some achieve a fresh perspective or broadening
of significance. The first half dozen might be seen as
concerning the act of creating art – poetry – the next few
concerned with women, the next with death. The group
starting with 'You, Never-arriving One' – immediately
after 'O This is the Animal that Cannot Be ' – and finish-
ing with 'The Convalescent' – might be said to trace the
arc of a love affair; giving significance to the poem after
them, 'Christ's Descent Into Hell', which begins "past
temptation at last...". Other poems are also linked by
theme and mood – identification with nature, a sense of
passive being in 'The Asylum Garden' and 'Look at the

Flowers' – moving through real and spiritual winters to new life and celebration in 'O Lacrimosa' and 'Be Ahead of All Parting'– but with Rilke this kind of categorisation and implied narrative is always elusive. Whatever the apparent subject matter of his poems the best create a transformative power which lifts object, theme or technical approach out of itself, or locates a deeper significance within itself, beyond expected boundaries. So rather than suggesting any defining relationship, this approach to arranging the poems is more a loose stringing together of the compatible, a highlighting of commonality, along with a juxtaposition of image and theme which might seem at first glance to be operating at entirely different levels – as in the case of 'The First Elegy' being followed by 'On the Verge of Night' for example. The implication is that the poems gain from being read in the order printed, but obviously this does not preclude opening the book at any page and dipping – all the poems are achieved works of art more than able to stand on their own.

Each being able to stand on its own as a fully-realised English language poem is the main criterion I have used when making these translations, alongside trying to indicate the essence of Rilke's sound, technique and sense. I have listened to his idiosyncratic voice, while bearing in mind that translating poetry from one language to another is an act of transformation itself; the poem becomes another voice's poem. I have made no attempt to try to be Rilke, or alternatively to aspire to an 'objectivity' which denies the truth that his words, and the perceptions and thoughts that animate them, are being filtered through the sieve of another time, language and sensibility. Any translation is a meeting and blend of voices – which explains why no two translations of a work are ever the same – and finding an appropriate balance between Rilke's and my own has been a constant and demanding pre-occupation.

I have chosen to make my versions as accessible as possible to today's readers of English, while retaining the complexity and, sometimes, radical inconclusiveness of the originals. Rhyming, metre, phrasing and sentence length all have a structural role to play in the shaping of both sound and the accumulated significance of a poem, so I have usually retained the shape, number and length of lines and, where possible, the phrase and sentence length of the originals. When Rilke uses rhyme he does so skilfully and, sometimes, obsessively. I have followed him, though frequently using half-rhyme for reasons of expediency, and also because his close full rhymes can seem to chime too insistently for modern ears. In one case – 'Love Song' – I have indulged in creating a new – obsessive – rhyme scheme which feels appropriate to the mood as well as being indicative of the kind of playfulness Rilke appears to have enjoyed. When he chooses not to rhyme – as he frequently does, particularly in longer poems – I have followed suit.

I have tried not to use what I referred to earlier as Rilke's 'radical inconclusiveness' – C. F. McIntyre calls it "purposed vagueness", David Oswald calls it "careful indeterminacy" – as a licence to take off anywhere. Where I have created some new metaphor, or taken a direction he does not take, it is to bring life and clarity to the apparent significance of the poetry for twenty-first century English language readers, not to deliberately replace or distort his thought or expression. I have sometimes changed from past to present tense to increase the immediacy of the poetry, and occasionally from third to first person for the same reason. Finally, I have provided brief notes at the end of the book to indicate where each poem fits in terms of Rilke's volumes of poetry. Where it seemed likely to facilitate the reader's way into a poem I have also added notes to some about the context and content.

Overall I hope this selection conveys something of Rilke's quirky and subtle sensibility, his largeness of heart and penetration of mind, and the transformative powers of his art. I hope too that readers new to Rilke will want to go on and explore more – there is so much – and that some seasoned Rilke-readers might find their perceptions of a poem or Rilke himself refreshed.

Ian Crockatt

Rose, oh reiner Widerspruch, Lust,
Niemandes Schlaf zu sein unter
soviel Lidern.

Rose, oh pure contradiction, joy,
in being nobody's sleep under
so many eyelids

*Rilke's self-penned epitaph, inscribed on his
gravestone in the churchyard at Raron, near Muzot.*

LE RUBAN

L'aurai-je exprimé, avant de m'en aller,
ce cœur qui, tourmenté, consent á être?
Étonnement sans fin, qui fus mon maître,
jusqu'à la fin t'aurai-je imité?

Mais tous surpasse comme un jour d'eté
le tender jeste qui trop tard admire;
dans nos paroles écloses, qui respire
le pur parfum d'identité?

Et cette belle qui s'en va, comment
la ferait en passer par une image?
Son doux ruban flottant vit davantage
que cette ligne qui s'éprend.

ICH LIEBE MEINES WESENS DUNKELSTUNDEN

Ich liebe meines Wesens Dunkelstunden,
in welchen meine Sinne sich vertiefen;
in ihnen hab ich, wie in alten Briefen,
mein täglich Leben schon gelebt gefunden
und wie Legende weit und überwunden.

Aus ihnen kommt mir Wissen, daß ich Raum
zu einum zweiten zeitlos breiten Leben habe.

Und manchmal bin ich wie der Baum,
der, reif und rauschend, über einem Grabe
den Traum erfüllt, den der vergangne Knabe
(um den sich seine warmen Wurzeln drängen)
verlor in Traurigkeiten und Gesängen.

THE RIBBON

Will I have expressed it before I go,
my tormented heart which consents to live?
Increasingly astonishment masters me –
will I have proved its equal before I leave?

But all surpasses, like a summer's day
your tender gesture compliments too late.
Is the pure perfume of identity
breathed in with the words we create?

And that departing beauty, how can
she be summed up by some metaphor?
Her frail ribbon floats with more élan
than this line does, which worships her.

I LOVE MY NATURE'S DARKEST HOURS

I love my nature's darkest hours,
those which fully engage my mind;
in them I've, as in ancient letters, found
my daily life already lived, with far-
seeing legends' overwhelming power.

From them comes the belief that I
have space for life's second, timeless span;

that sometimes, like a tree
ripe and rustling over a grave, I *can*
fulfil the dream that boy long gone
(round whom its warm roots still cling)
lost to sadness and song.

EINGANG

Wer du auch seist: am Abend tritt hinaus
aus deiner Stube, drin du alles weißt;
als letzes vor der Ferne liegt dein Haus:
wer du auch seist.
Mit deinen Augen, welche müde kaum
von der verbrauchten Schwelle sich befrein,
hebst du ganz langsam einen schwarzen Baum
und stellst ihn vor den Himmel: schlank, allein.
Und hast die Welt gemacht. Und sie ist groß
und wie ein Wort, das noch im Schweigen reift.
Und wie dein Wille ihren Sinn begreift,
lassen sie deine Augen zärtlich los…

FRÜHER APOLLO

Wie manches Mal durch das noch unbelaubte
Gezweig ein Morgen durchsieht, der schon ganz
im Frühling ist: so ist in seinem Haupte
nichts vas verhindern könnte, daß der Glanz

aller Gedichte uns fast tödlich träfe;
denn noch kein Schatten ist in seinem Schaun,
zu kühl für Lorbeer sind noch seine Schläfe
und später erst wird aus den Augenbraun

hochstämmig sich der Rosengarten heben
aus welchem Blätter, einzeln, ausgelöst
hintreiben werden auf des Mundes Beben,

der jetzt noch still ist, niegebraucht und blinkend
und nur mit seinem Lächeln etwas trinkend
als würde ihm sein Singen eingeflößt.

ENTRANCE

Whoever you are; step out of your familiar
room into the evening. Your house
is the last before the endless.
Whoever you are.
With your tired eyes, scarcely able to
look beyond the time-worn threshold, you
raise a dark tree up, slowly,
and stand it against the sky; frail, solitary.
And you have made the world; it is tall,
and like a word it ripens in silence.
And as your will absorbs its significance
your eyes allow it, tenderly, to fall…

EARLY APOLLO

As if a precocious spring dawn
had arrived ahead of itself and cast fire
amongst the naked trees, this simple stone
head utterly exposes us to the core,

to the fatal blood-sweet clamour of poetry.
He looks us straight and fresh in the eye
and his brow is too young to have earned praise; though
it's not too hard to conceive those lyrical roses, high-

stemmed and perfumed, sprouting out of it, petal
after petal loosed from his eyebrows falling
as tender rain to his lips, subtle

as kisses on his unawakened mouth,
which trembles, half-smiling, as if new truths
were tempting it with unbearably pure song.

LA FONTAINE

Je ne veux qu'une seule leçon, c'est la tienne,
fontaine, qui en toi-même retombes –
celle des eaux risquées auxquelles incombe
ce céleste retour vers la vie terrienne.

Autant que ton multiple murmure
rien ne saurait me server d'exemple;
toi, ô colonne légère du temple
qui se détruit par sa propre nature.

Dans ta chute, combien se module
chaque jet d'eau qui termine sa danse.
Que je me sens l'élève, l'émule
de ton innombrable nuance!

Mais ce qui plus que ton chant vers toi me décide
c'est cet instant d'un silence en délire
lorsqu' à la nuit, à travers ton élan liquide
passe ton propre retour qu'un souffle retire.

DA STIEG EIN BAUM. O REINE ÜBERSTEIGUNG!

Da stieg ein Baum. O reine Übersteigung!
O Orpheus singt! O hoher Baum im Ohr!
Und alles schwieg. Doch selbst in der Verschweigung
ging neuer Anfang, Wink und Wandlung vor.

Tiere aus stille drangen aus dem klaren
gelösten Wald von Lager und Genist;
und da ergab sich, daß sie nicht aus List
und nicht aus Angst in sich so leise waren,

THE FOUNTAIN

I want only one lesson – yours,
fountain falling back into yourself; whose waters
are committed to risking all
on this return to the earthly from the celestial.

There is no better example
than your many-voiced murmur;
you, O slender column of the temple
to whom self-destruction is nature.

How each jet of water modulates
itself as it falls at the end of the dance.
How like a student I feel, who imitates
your every uncountable nuance.

But what persuades me even more than your singing
is that one instant of feverish silence,
at night, like an indrawn breath, when, returning,
you pass through your own liquid resurgence.

A TREE ROSE UP – O PURE TRANSCENDENCE!

A tree rose up – O pure transcendence!
Orpheus sings – O tall tree in the ear!
The world stood still – in that silence
the new began, gestures changed, all altered.

Creatures of stillness pushed eagerly out
of the lit-up wood, left holt and nest and lair.
It wasn't incomprehension, or fear,
which made them so inwardly quiet –

sondern aus Hören. Brüllen, Schrei, Geröhr
schien klein in ihren Herzen. Und wo eben
kaum eine Hütte war, dies zu empfangen,

ein Unterschlupf aus dunkelstem Verlangen
mit einem Zugang, dessen Pfosten beben –
da schufst du ihnen Tempel im Gehör.

DIE GAZELLE

Gazella Dorcas

Verzauberte: wie kann der Einklang zweier
erwählter Worte je den Reim erreichen,
der in dir kommt und geht, wie auf ein Zeichen.
Aus deiner Stirne steigen Laub und Leier,

Und alles Deine geht schon im Vergleich
durch Liebeslieder, deren Worte, weich
wie Rosenblätter, dem, der nicht mehr liest,
sich auf die Augen legen, die er schließt:

um dich zu sehen: hingetragen, als
wäre mit Sprüngen jeder Lauf geladen
und schösse nur nicht ab, solang der Hals

das Haupt ins Horchen hält: wie wenn beim Baden
im Wald die Badende sich unterbricht:
den Waldsee im gewendeten Gesicht.

they were listening. Bellows, shrieks and roars
seemed to shrink in their hearts, and where that hut
hung in which they could scarcely receive song –

just a refuge for their obscurest desires,
an entry propped shakily upright –
you founded your temple, deep inside their hearing.

THE GAZELLE

Gazella Dorcas

Lyrical one: what two words, however true,
however exactingly spaced in the music of the poem,
could achieve the enchanted rhymes your limbs do?
Imagine this – your branched horns as lyres and from them

pouring, as from your muscles' natural moves,
a poetry so passionately infused
with wild rose that real petals form – which lie
with sweet hypnotic weight on the reader's eyes

till they close: and there *you* stand, legs
like loaded rifles, taut with unleapt leaps, listening;
as a girl, stock-still in a forest pool, begs

her heart to stop while she listens, naked,
hearing – or does she? – the undergrowth rustling,
her face, lit by the water, averted.

SPANISCHE TÄNZERIN

Wie in der Hand ein Schwefelzündholz, weiß,
eh es zur Flamme kommt, nach allen Seiten
zuckende Zungen streckt –: beginnt im Kreis
naher Beschauer hastig, hell und heiß
ihr runder Tanz sich zuckend auszubreiten.

Und plötzlich ist er Flamme, ganz und gar.

Mit einem Blick entzündet sie ihr Haar
und dreht auf einmal mit gewagter Kunst
ihr ganzes Kleid in diese Feuersbrunst,
aus welcher sich, wie Schlangen die erschrecken,
die nackten Arme wach und klappernd strecken.

Und dann: als würde ihr das Feuer knapp,
nimmt sie es ganz zusamm und wirft es ab
sehr herrisch, mit hochmütiger Gebärde
und schaut: da liegt es rasend auf der Erde
und flammt noch immer und ergiebt sich nicht –
Doch sieghaft, sicher und mit einem süßen
Grüßenden Lächeln hebt sie ihr Gesicht
und stampft es aus mit kleinen festen Füßen.

GEBURT DER VENUS

An diesem Morgen nach der Nacht, die bang
vergangen war mit Rufen, Unruh, Aufruhr, –
brach alles Meer noch einmal auf und schrie.
Und als der Schrei sich langsam wieder schloß

SPANISH DANCER

What struck match ever flared
so whitely from its core? Or shot
such flame-tongues out to lap the air? Or so seared
the faces of the crowd packed tightly round her,
their scorched lungs gasping for more? What

is this dance that turns a woman to fire?

A flick of her wrist and she's flames for hair,
one spin of her skirts inspires an inferno
of catherine-wheels, and out of them rise two
twining cobras of smoke, her undulating arms;
and there's noise – the clacking of castanets, applause
    becoming a storm –

then as quickly she halts and throws the whole blaze down,
with a high gesture of disdain,
like a lover unpeeling her basque and casting it,
seething with heat, to the floor. Now beat by beat
she brazenly sways and moves in for the kill.
She taunts mere flame – how dare it draw breath? –
and her face framed by her arms exults as the drum-roll
of her feet crescendos and she stamps fire to death.

BIRTH OF VENUS

Listen – after a night of fear, tumult and outrage,
of ocean, sky and aching Earth being torn open –
stillness. Oh but suddenly, one last time,
a wave parts its cold white lips and screams, screams.
Don't you see, wherever that scream is felt it withers life?

und von der Himmel blassem Tag und Anfang
herabfiel in der stummen Fische Abgrund – :
gebar das Meer.

Von erster Sonne schimmerte der Haarschaum
der weiten Woganscham, an deren Rand
das Mädchen aufstand, weiß, verwirrt and feucht.
So wie ein junges grünes Blatt sich rührt
sich reckt und Eingerolltes langsam aufschlägt,
entfaltete ihr Lieb sich in die Kühle
hinein und in den unberührten Frühwind.

Wie Monde stiegen klar die Kniee auf
und tauchten in der Schenkel Wolkenränder;
der Waden schmaler Schatten wich zurück,
die Füße spannten sich und wurden licht,
und die Gelenke lebten wie die Kehlen
von Trinkenden.

Und in dem Kelch des Beckens lag der Leib
wie eine junge Frucht in eines Kindes Hand.
In seines Nabels engem Becher war
Das ganze Dunkel dieses hellen Lebens.
Darunter hob sich Licht die kleine Welle
und floß beständig über nach den Lenden,
wo dann und wann ein stilles Rieseln war.
Durchschienen aber und noch ohne Schatten,
wie ein Bestand von Birken im April,
warm, leer und unverborgen, lag die Scham.

Jetzt stand der Schultern rege Waage schon
im Gleichgewichte auf dem graden Körper,
der aus dem Becken wie ein Springbrunn aufstieg
und zögernd in den langen Armen abfiel
und rascher in dem vollen Fall des Haars.

And yet when at last it subsides with the pale sky into
those fish-haunted fathoms
life happens.

A girl – out of the ocean's wave-wisped
fathomless sex there rises a glistening girl,
tiptoeing the chilly foam-curls, drenched, confused.
You have seen a young fern's dewy
uncoiling in cold spring light? So she
unfolds her untried nakedness into the breeze
shyly, as if testing the feel of this world.

And I know you have seen the bright moon's disc
ease gracefully into cloud – so her knees merge with her thighs.
Know that the curves of her shadowed calves
meet the foam-splashed tracery of her feet
with all firm gentleness, that each limb's inner movement's
like a slim throat swallowing wine.

Ah, let me tell how the young fruit of her belly
lies in the porcelain pelvic bowl
as in a child's hand, how the navel's
narrow well is the only night her sunlit skin has known.
Except – beneath the down-curve of her loins
where sometimes ripples rise, where the exposed torso
falls to the fork of the thighs, where, bared,
with the innocence of pale birches caught by April sun,
the dark notch of her sex draws all eyes.

She is a fountain, waist and pale scooped sides
rising from her hips to the balanced shoulders
then curving into the down-flow of the arms, before
cascading down again with her streaming hair;
upright yet falling, alive with all life.

Dann ging sehr langsam das Gesicht vorbei:
aus dem verkürzten Dunkel seiner Neigung
in klares, waagrechtes Erhobensein.
Und hinter ihm verschloß sich steil das Kinn.

Jetzt, da der Hals gestreckt war wie ein Strahl
und wie ein Blumenstiel, darin der Saft steigt,
streckten sich auch die Arme aus wie Hälse
von Schwänen, wenn sie nach dem Ufer suchen.

Dann kam in dieses Liebes dunkle Frühe
wie Morgenwind der erste Atemzug.
Im zartesten Geäst der Aderbäume
enstand ein Flüstern, und das Blut begann
zu rauschen über seinen tiefen Stellen.
Und dieser Wind wuchs an: nun warf er sich
mit allem Atem in die neuen Brüste
und füllte sie und drückte sich in sie, –
das sie wie Segel, von der Ferne voll,
das leichte Mädchen nach dem Strande drängten.

So landete die Göttin.

Hinter ihr,
die rasch dahinschritt durch die jungen Ufer,
erhoben sich den ganzen Vormittag
die Blumen and die Halme, warm, verwirrt,
wie aus Umarmung. Und sie ging und lief.

Am Mittag aber, in der schwersten Stunde,
hob sich das Meer noch einmal auf und warf
einen Delphin an jene selbe Stelle.
Tot, rot und offen.

How can we hope to fully know the face,
still ocean-rapt? Yet now it is quietly raised
to look, held high and horizontal –
see how it falls to the firm abbreviation of the chin,

and how the neck's stretched sunbeam,
its sap-filled flower-stalk length,
echoes the reaching arms which stretch
like twin swans' necks seeking their shore.

Imagine her first air-breath as the original dawn breeze,
that first inhalation of new life – and how
the whispering blood engorges every vein,
spurts through each tendril and branch
until it thunders through the sluices of the heart;
and the breeze of her breath becoming a wind
that fills her, swells her timid breasts
till they are sails filling with distance,
drawing her over the waves, faster, driving her
on, till at last she stumbles ashore.

Just to see you, Goddess, on that beach

strolling your new-found land, all
the confused grasses and flowers in your wake springing up
as if from loving, warm with abandoned embraces – you,
walking and running, glad of your life, this world.

Then, at noon, Earth's heaviest hour,
the ocean opens its maw again
and spews up onto that very beach
a dolphin; dead, red, gaping.

AUSGESETZT AUF DEN BERGEN DES HERZENS.

Ausgesetzt auf den Bergen des Herzens. Siehe, wie klein dort,
siehe: die letzte Ortschaft der Worte, und höher,
aber wie klein auch, noch ein letztes
Gehöft von Gefühl. Erkennst du's?
Ausgesetzt auf den Bergen des Herzens. Steingrund
unter den Händen. Hier blüht wohl
einiges auf; aus stummem Absturz
blüht ein unwissendes Kraut singend hervor.
Aber der Wissende? Ach, der zu wissen begann
und schweigt nun, ausgesetzt auf den Bergen des Herzens.
Da geht wohl, heilen Bewußtseins,
manches umher, manches gesicherte Bergtier,
wechselt und weilt. Und der große geborgene Vogel
kreist um der Gipfel reine Verweigerung. – Aber
ungeborgen, hier auf den Bergen des Herzens…

'MAN MUSS STERBEN WEIL MAN SIE KENNT'

*Papyrus prisse, aus den Sprüchen des Ptah-hetep,
Handschrift um 2000 v. ch.*

'Man muß sterben weil man sie kennt'. Sterben
an der unsäglichen Blüte des Lächelns. Sterben
an ihren leichten Händen. Sterben
an Frauen.

Singe der Jüngling die tödlichen,
wenn sie ihm hoch durch den Herzraum
wandeln. Aus seiner blühenden Brust
sing er sie an:
unerreichbare! Ach wie sie fremd sind.
Über den Gipfeln

EXPOSED ON THE MOUNTAINS OF THE HEART

Exposed on the mountains of the heart. Look, how small there,
look: the last village of words, and, higher,
and even smaller, one last
farmstead of feeling – do you know it?
Exposed on the mountains of the heart. Bedrock
under your hands yet
something still blooms here, from the soundless precipice
an unknowing plant blossoms and sings out.
But what of the knowing? Ah, we who began to know
are silent now, exposed on the mountains of the heart.
At ease with themselves, and fully alert,
many an untroubled mountain beast
passes, or lingers. And the great invulnerable bird
circles the peaks of pure denial. But
vulnerable, here on the mountains of the heart…

'WE MUST DIE BECAUSE WE KNOW THEM'

*Papyrus Prisse. From the saying of Ptah-Hotep, Manuscript
from circa 2000 BC.*

"We must die because we know them". Die
of their smiles' indescribable bloom. Die
of their light hands. Die
of women.

Sing, young man, as they make their fatal way
through your high-vaulted heart;
let it blossom in your breast
and sing out to them –
Unreachable Ones! Ah, how far beyond us you are.
Above the peaks of our feeling

seines Gefühls gehn sie hervor und ergießen
süß verwandelte Nacht ins verlassene
Tal seine Arme. Es rauscht
wind ihres Aufgangs im Laub seines Leibes. Es glänzen
seine Bäche dahin.

Aber der Mann
schweige erschütterter. Er, der
pfadlos die Nacht im Gebirg
seiner Gefühle geirrt hat:
schweige.

Wie der Seemann schweigt, der ältere,
und die bestandenen
Schrecken spielen in ihm wie in zitternden Käfigen.

DICH, DIE ICH KANNTE WIE EINE BLUME

Dich, aber will ich nun, *Dich*, die ich kannte
wie eine Blume, von der ich den Namen nicht weiß,
noch *ein* Mal erinnern und ihnen zeigen, Entwandte,
schöne Gespielin des unüberwindlichen Schrei's.

Tänzerin erst, die plötzlich, den Körper voll Zögern,
anhielt, als göß man ihr Jungsein in Erz;
trauernd und lauschend – . Da, von den hohen Vermögern
fiel ihr Musik in das veränderte Herz.

Nah war die Krankheit. Schon von den Schatten bemächtigt,
drängte verdunkelt das Blut, doch, wie flüchtig verdächtigt,
trieb es in seinen natürlichen Frühling hervor.

you issue forth and pour
night's transfiguring sweetness into the desolate
valleys of our arms. The wind
of your rising rustles every leaf of our bodies, their streams
go glittering on their way.

Yet we are silent,
utterly shaken; isn't every man
who has lost his path at night
in the mountain-range of his feelings
silent?

As the long-retired sailor is silent,
the terrors he went through
still playing in him as though in quivering cages.

YOU, WHOM I KNEW LIKE A FLOWER

But you, whom I knew like a flower
I could not name, you who were taken so early,
I'll conjure up your image and show them once more,
you, lovely companion of the inconsolable cry.

First a dancer; then your body, gripped by hesitation,
stops: like a bronze cast of your young-girl-ness;
listens and grieves; until god-given
music falls to your altered heart. Now illness

grows. Overwhelmed by shadows, yet still only
passingly concerned, your blood, flowing darkly,
rushes you into your natural Spring.

Wieder und wieder, von Dunkel and Sturz unterbrochen,
glänzte es irdisch. Bis es nach schrecklichem Pochen
trat in das trostlos offene Tor.

LEICHEN-WÄSCHE

Sie hatten sich an ihn gewöhnt. Doch als
die Küchenlampe kam und unruhig brannte
im dunkeln Luftzug, war der Unbekannte
ganz unbekannt. Sie wuschen seinen Hals,

und da sie nichts von seinem Schicksal wußten,
so logen sie ein anderes zusamm,
fortwährend waschend. Eine mußte husten
und leiß solang den schweren Essigschwamm

auf dem Gesicht. Da gab es eine Pause
auch für die zweite. Aus der harten Bürste
klopften die Tropfen: während seine grause
gekrampfte Hand dem ganzen Hause
beweisen wollte, daß ihn nicht mehr dürste.

Und er bewies. Sie nahmen wie betreten
eiliger jetzt mit einem kurzen Huster
die Arbeit auf, so daß an den Tapeten
ihr krummer Schatten in dem stummen Muster

sich wand und wälzte wie in einem Netze,
bis daß die Waschenden zu Ende kamen.
Die Nacht im vorhanglosen Fensterrahmen
war rücksichtslos. Und einer ohne Namen
lag bar und reinlich da und gab Gesetze.

Again and again darkness and negation disrupted
its earthly brilliance. Until, horribly corrupted,
it poured through that door's dismal opening.

WASHING THE CORPSE

*Of course we are accustomed to death. But when
the kitchen lamp splutters and smokes in a draught,
and darkness throws itself about the room, and a waft
from the unknown corpse washes over you, your mouth, your skin…*

They scoured the stranger's neck, coarsely laughing
at the farce-life they invented
to contain him, hamming it up on his breast till one mock-fainted.
The other, doubled up and coughing,

propping her vinegar-sponge against the nose,
couldn't go on. They paused. Some water-drops
from her stiff brush pooled at the base
of his chest. They saw his contorted hand's crass
last grasp at words – a cramped gesture that croaked "stop,

I no longer thirst". They heard. Uneasily now,
clearing their throats, they got on with it,
stooping beneath their own monstrous shadows
which reeled on the patterned walls as if they were caught,
frightened and thrashing, in a net.

*We sponged and scrubbed till his numb limbs gleamed.
Implacable night bloomed through the window-frame.
Suddenly the naked nameless one's loom
pulsed, then swept like a lighthouse's round the room.*

REQUIEM FÜR EINE FREUNDIN

Ich habe Tote, und ich ließ sie hin
und war estaunt, sie so getrost zu sehn,
so rasch zuhaus im Totsein, so gerecht,
so anders als ihr Ruf. Nur du, du kehrst
zurück; du streifst mich, du gehst um, du willst
an etwas stoßen, daß es klingt von dir
und dich verrät. O nimm mir nicht, was ich
langsam erlern. Ich habe recht; du irrst
wenn du gerührt zu irgend einem Ding
ein Heimweh hast. Wir wandeln dieses um;
es is nicht hier, wir spiegeln es herein
aus unserm Sein, sobald wir es erkennen.
    Ich glaubte dich viel weiter. Mich verwirrts,
daß *du* gerade irrst und kommst, die mehr
verwandelt hat als irgend eine Frau.
Daß wir erschracken, da du starbst, nein, daß
dein starker Tod uns dunkel unterbrach,
das Bisdahin abreißend von Seither:
das geht uns an; das einzuordnen wird
die Arbeit sein, die wir mit allem tun.
Doch daß du selbst erschrakst und auch noch jetzt
den Schrecken hast, wo Schrecken nicht mehr gilt;
daß du von deiner Ewigkeit ein Stück
verlierst und hier hereintrittst, Freundin, hier,
wo alles noch nicht *ist*; daß du zerstreut,
zum ersten Mal im All zerstreut und halb,
den Aufgang der unendlichen Naturen
nicht so ergriffst wie hier ein jedes Ding;
daß aus dem Kreislauf, der dich schon empfing,
die stumme Schwerkraft irgend einer Unruh
dich niederzieht zur abgezählten Zeit – :
dies weckt mich nachts oft wie ein Dieb, der einbricht.
Und dürft ich sagen, daß du nur geruhst,
daß du aus Großmut kommt, aus Überfülle,
weil du so sicher bist, so in dir selbst,

I have my dead. I have let them go
and been astonished to see them at ease,
so quickly at home in their deaths, so justified,
so at odds with their reputation. Only you,
you turn back; you who brush against me, hang around,
would knock against things so that the noise
gives you away: O don't take away
what I've taken so long to learn. I'm right; and you are
mistaken if you allow yourself homesickness
for even one Thing; we change Things,
they are not here, as soon as we recognize them
we make them shiny reflections of our selves.
    I thought you had progressed further. I'm confused,
that you of all people have wandered back, you
who had already transformed yourself
so much more than other women. It's not
that we were frightened when you died – rather
your powerful death darkly burst in on us,
tearing 'what-will-be' from 'what-once-was'.
That is *our* concern: – making sense of it all
is the work we have always before us.
But that you also had fears, are still fearful,
when fear can no longer have validity for you;
that you have lost a portion of your eternity
and re-appear here, my friend, here
where all is still nothing; that you, absent-minded,
for the first time unfocused, did not
immediately seize the promise of infinite nature,
that the silent gravity of some imbalance
has drawn you down from the cycles which had
received you, back into linear time: – so often
this wakes me at night, like a burglar breaking in.
If I could say "she condescends", or "she comes
out of magnanimity, sheer abundance", or
"it's because she is so certain, so rooted in herself",

daß du herumgehst wie ein Kind, nicht bange
vor Örtern, wo man einem etwas tut – :
doch nein: du bittest. Dieses geht mir so
bis ins Gebein und querrt wie ein Säge.
Ein Vorwurf, den du trügest als Gespenst,
nachtrügest mir, wenn ich mich nachts zurückzieh
in meine Lunge, in die Eingeweide,
in meines Herzens letzte ärmste Kammer, –
ein solcher Vorwurf wäre nicht so grausam,
wie dieses Bitten ist. Was bittest du?

Sag, soll ich reisen? Hast du irgendwo
ein Ding zurückgelassen, das sich quält
und das dir nachwill? Soll ich in ein Land,
das du nicht sahst, obwohl es dir verwandt
war wie die andre Hälfte deiner Sinne?

...

Dann aber will ich, wenn ich vieles weiß,
einfach die Tiere anschaun, daß ein Etwas
von ihrer Wendung mir in die Gelenke
herübergleitet; will ein kurzes Dasein
in ihren Augen haben, die mich halten
und langsam lassen, ruhig, ohne Urteil.
Ich will mir von den Gärtnern viele Blumen
hersagen lassen, daß ich in den Scherben
der schönen Eigennamen einen Rest
herüberbringe von der hundert Düften.
Und Früchte will ich kaufen, Früchte, drin
das Land noch einmal ist, bis an dem Himmel.
Denn Das verstandest du: die vollen Früchte.
Die legtest du auf Schalen vor dich hin
und wogst mit Farben ihre Schwere auf.
Und so wie Früchte sahst du auch die Fraun
und sahst die Kinder so, von innen her

even "these are the wanderings of a child, afraid
of nothing and nowhere"; but no, you are
pleading: – Oh this penetrates right to the bone,
cuts through me like a saw.
As a ghost, any reproach you might bring me,
might make me endure at night when I retreat
into my lungs, into my gut, into the last
most naked chamber of my heart –
no such reproach could be as cruel as
this pleading. What is it you plead for? –
      Tell me. Should I travel? Have you left some Thing
behind somewhere that is tortured by longing for you?
Should I travel to that land you never saw, although
it was as closely related to you as
the other side of your mind…

      …
                                          I will
simply look at animals, and let something
of their essence glide into my limbs; I
will briefly exist in their eyes, which will
lingeringly hold me then let me go,
quietly, unjudged. I will have gardeners
come and name me flower on flower,
and from the small sounds of their proper names
glean glimmers of their hundred fragrances.
And I will buy fruit, fruit in which you can
still taste the land and, yes, the sky.

      For this you understood – ripe fruit.
You placed fruit in bowls before you
and measured the heaviness of its colours.
And it was as fruits too that you saw women;
and also children, growing from the inside

getrieben in die Formen ihres Daseins.
Und sahst dich selbst zuletzt wie eine Frucht,
nahmst dich heraus aus deinen Kleidern, trugst
dich vor den Spiegel, ließest dich hinein
bis auf dein Schauen; das blieb groß davor
und sagte nicht: das bin ich; nein; dies ist.
So ohne Neugier war zuletzt dein Schaun
und so besitzlos, von so wahrer Armut,
daß es dich selbst nicht mehr begehrte; heilig.

So will ich dich behalten, wie du dich
hinstelltest in den Spiegel, tief hinein
und fort von allem.

   ...

Komm her ins Kerzenlicht. Ich bin nicht bang,
die Toten anzuschauen. Wenn sie kommen,
so haben sie ein Recht, in unserm Blick
sich aufzuhalten, wie die andern Dinge.

Komm her; wir wollen eine Weile still sein.
Sieh diese Rose an auf meinem Schreibtisch;
ist nicht das Licht um sie genau so zaghaft
wie über dir: sie dürfte auch nicht hier sein.
Im Garten draußen, unvermischt mit mir,
hätte sie bleiben müssen oder hingehn, –
nun währt sie so: was ist ihr mein Bewußtsein?

Erschrick nicht, wenn ich jetzt begreife, ach,
da steigt es in mir auf: ich kann nicht anders,
ich muß begreifen, und wenn ich dran stürbe.
Begreifen, daß du hier bist. Ich begreife.
Ganz wie ein Blinder rings ein Ding begreift,
fühl ich dein Los und weiß ihm keinen Namen.
Laß uns zusammen klagen, daß dich einer
aus deinem Spiegel nahm. Kannst du noch weinen?

into their destined shapes. Finally
you saw yourself as a fruit; you let your clothes
drop from you, positioned yourself
in front of the mirror and allowed yourself
to become your gaze in it; which stayed
unflinchingly before you and did not say
"that's me; no, this is."
At last your gaze was so incurious, so
un-possessive, of such true poverty,
that it no longer desired; not even you. Holy.
     And that is how I will remember you –
as you placed yourself in front of the mirror, deep
within it, far gone from all this…

     …

Come into the candlelight. I'm not afraid
to look on the dead. When they come they have
as much right as other Things to be scrutinised by us.
     Come. Let's make a moment of quietness together.
Look at this rose on my desk – isn't
the timid light that surrounds it uncannily
similar to yours? It shouldn't be here either,
it should be outdoors in the garden, not
mixed up with me, having to both fade and remain.
Meanwhile it *is* – but what can my awareness mean to it?
     Don't be alarmed if I understand it now – ah,
it's flowering is in me. I have no choice
but to grasp it, even if it might prove
the death of me. Must grasp that you *are* here;
as a blind man, groping about, grasps something,
I feel your fate but cannot name it. Come,
let's mourn together – that someone plucked
you from the mirror. Can you still cry?

Du kannst nicht. Deiner Tränen Kraft und Andrang
hast du verwandelt in dein reifes Anschaun
und warst dabei, jeglichen Saft in dir
so umzusetsen in ein starkes Dasein,
das steigt und kreist, im Gleichgewicht und blindlings.
Da riß ein Zufall dich, dein letzer Zufall
riß dich zurück aus deinem fernsten Fortschritt
in eine Welt zurück, wo Säfte *wollen*.

...

Wenn du noch da bist, wenn in diesem Dunkel
noch eine Stelle ist, an der dein Geist
empfindlich mitschwingt auf den flachen Schallwelln,
die eine Stimme, einsam in der Nacht,
aufregt in eines hohen Zimmers Strömung:
So hör mich: Hilf mir. Sieh, wir gleiten so,
nicht wissend wann, zurück aus unserm Fortschritt
in irgendwas, was wir nicht meinen; drin
wir uns verfangen wie in einem Traum
und drin wir sterben, ohne zu erwachen.
Keiner ist weiter. Jedem, der sein Blut
hinaufhob in ein Werk, das lange wird,
kann es geschehen, daß ers nicht mehr hochhält
und daß es geht nach seiner Schwere, wertlos.
Denn irgendwo ist eine alte Feindschaft
zwischen dem Leben und der großen Arbeit.
Daß ich sie einseh und sie sage: hilf mir.
    Komm nicht zurück. Wenn du's erträgst, so sei
tot bei den Toten. Tote sind beschäftigt.
Doch hilf mir so, daß es dich nicht zerstreut,
wie mir das Fernste manchmal hilft: in mir.

You can't. You transferred your tears' pressure
and strength into your ripe gaze,
transformed every other fluid in you
into more enduring substance which would
blindly rise and circulate in a new symmetry.
Then chance dragged you back, one last time
tore you back into the world where flesh
insists, back from your soul's furthest advance…

   …

If you are still there, if there is still a place
in this darkness where your sensitive soul
vibrates on the shallow sound-waves
of a solitary voice in the night –
sustained by the high room's acoustics –
hear me; help me. See, we slip back
so easily, imperceptibly, from
what progress we have made into ways
we would not choose; find ourselves caught
as in a dream, and die without ever waking.
No-one is beyond this; it can happen
to anyone whose blood is committed
to some lengthy undertaking, that he can no longer
sustain it, and its gravity pulls him down. Worthless.
For somewhere there is an age-old enmity
between living life and making great work.
Help me to recognize this, and say it.
Don't come back. If you can endure it, be
dead with the dead. The dead have their work too.
So help me, if you can without breaking up,
for what is most distant from me can help. In me.

DER TOD

Da steht der Tod, ein bläulicher Absud
in einer Tasse ohne Untersatz.
Ein wunderlicher Platz für eine Tasse:
steht auf dem Rücken einer Hand. Ganz gut
erkennt man noch an dem glasierten Schwung
den Bruch des Henkels. Staubig. Und: *Hoff-nung*
an ihrem Bug in aufgebrauchter Schrift.

Das hat der Trinker, den der Trank betrifft,
bei einem fernen Frühstück ab-gelesen.

Was sind den das für Wesen,
die man zuletzt wegschrecken muß mit Gift?

Blieben sie sonst? Sind sie den hier vernarrt
in dieses Essen voller Hindernis?
Man muß ihnen die harte Gegenwart
ausnehmen, wie ein künstliches Gebiß.
Dann lallen sie. Gelall, Gelall…

        …

O Sternenfall,
von einer Brücke einmal eingesehn – :
Dich nicht vergessen. Stehn!

DEATH

There stands death; a bluish liquor
in a saucerless cup. Odd
place for a cup indeed –
it stands on the back of a hand. The fracture
where the handle met the glazed
curve can clearly be discerned. Dusty. Faded
script around its lip spelling HO-PE.

Whoever was the drinker who drank from that cup,
at a breakfast long past, must have read it out loud.

So what kind of people end up
scared out of here by poison? Would

they have stayed otherwise? Are they addicted
enough to keep swallowing the unpalatable here?
The hardness of this life must be extracted
from them, like false teeth – then they slur

and babble, slapgum, slapslaver…

   …

O shooting star
once glimpsed from a bridge, then gone.
Not to forget you. Hold on!

KLAGE

O wie is alles fern
und lange vergangen.
Ich glaube, der Stern,
von welchem ich Glanz empfange,
ist seit Jahrtausenden tot.
Ich glaube, im Boot,
das vorüberfuhr,
hörte ich etwas Banges sagen.
Im Hause hat eine Uhr
geschlagen…
In welchem Haus?…
Ich möchte aus meinem Herzen hinaus
unter den großen Himmel treten.
Ich möchte beten.
Und einer von allen Sternen
müste wirklich noch sein.
Ich glaube, ich wüßte,
welcher allein
gedauert hat, –
welcher wie eine weiße Stadt
am Ende des Strahls in den Himmeln steht…

UND FAST EIN MÄDCHEN WARS

Und fast ein Mädchen wars und ging hervor
aus diesem einigen Glück von Sang und Leier
und glänzte klar durch ihre Frühlingsschleier
und machte sich ein Bett in meinem Ohr.

Und schlief in mir. Und alles war ihr Schlaf.
Die Bäume, die ich je bewundert, diese

LAMENT

O everything is distant
and long over.
I believe that brilliant
star is dead; its lustre
has taken us in for thousands of years.
I believe it was fear
I heard in that passing boat,
terrible, articulate.
A clock struck
in a house…
but which house?
I long to walk
out of my heart into
the huge sky,
I long to pray.
Surely out of all
these stars one is real?
I believe I know
which one – see,
it stands like a white city
at the end of its beam in the sky.

AND IT WAS A GIRL, ALMOST

And it was a girl almost, who, born
of the joyful coincidence of voice and lyre,
and shining nakedly through spring's soft veils, turned
my ear into a final bed for her

and slept in me. Her sleep was everything:
the enthralled trees, the immeasurably

fühlbare Ferne, die gefühlte Wiese
und jedes Staunen, das mich selbst betraf.

Sie schlief die Welt. Singender Gott, wie hast
du sie vollendet, daß sie nicht begehrte,
erst wach zu sein? Sieh, sie erstand und schlief.

Wo ist ihr Tod? O, wirst du dies Motiv
erfinden noch, eh sich dein Lied verzehrte? –
Wo sinkt sie hin aus mir?… Ein Mädchen fast…

ORPHEUS. EURYDIKE. HERMES.

Das war der Seelen wunderliches Bergwerk.
Wie stille Silbererze gingen sie
als Adern durch sein Dunkel. Zwischen Wurzeln
entsprang das Blut, das fortgeht zu den Menschen,
und schwer wie Porphyr sah es aus im Dunkel.
Sonst war nichts Rotes.

Felsen waren da
und wesenlose Wälder. Brücken über Leeres
und jener große graue blinde Teich,
der über seinem fernen Grunde hing
wie Regenhimmel über einer Landschaft.
Und zwischen Wiesen, sanft und voller Langmut,
erschien des einen Weges blasser Streifen,
wie eine lange Bleiche hingelegt.

deep distances, the meadows of pure feeling –
all the world's wonders overwhelmed me.

She slept the world – O God of Song have we lost
that original sleep from which we longed
never to wake? See, she rises, she sleeps.

Where is her death? Will you make and weep
her elegy, which is your own song's dying?
How far must she sink from me?… A girl, almost…

ORPHEUS. EURYDICE. HERMES.

It was her heart's deep soul-mine.
They followed silvered veins of ore
through its echoing darkness. Gouts
of arterial blood welled up between black roots,
red-rich as porphyry, rock-hard,
which once rose up as fountains
to feed the living limbs and brain above.
Nothing more was red,

though all she had imagined was there.
Mysterious forests shouldered their frightened silence;
crumblings of rock spanned chasms
over which they must walk. High in the distance
the blind, grey, swaying underbelly
of a lake hung over its bed
like a premonition of thunder over the fields –
through which there wound a pale dropped bandage, their path.

Und dieses einen Weges kamen sie.

Voran der schlanke Mann im blauen Mantel,
der stumm und ungeduldig vor sich aussah.
Ohne zu kauen fraß sein Schritt den Weg
in großen Bissen; seine Hände hingen
schwer und verschlossen aus dem Fall der Falten
und wußten nicht mehr von der leichten Leier,
die in die Linke eingewaschen war
wie Rosenranken in den Ast des Ölbaums.
Und seine Sinne waren wie entzweit:
indes der Blick ihm wie ein Hund vorauslief,
umkehrte, kam und immer wieder weit
und wartend an der nächsten Wendung stand –
blieb sein Gehör wie ein Geruch zurück.
Manchmal erschien es ihm als reichte es
bis an das Gehen jener beiden andern,
die folgen sollten diesen ganzen Aufstieg.
Dann wieder war nur seines Steigens Nachklang
und seines Mantels Wind was hinter ihm var.
Er aber sagte sich, sie kämen doch:
sagte es laut und hörte sich verhallen.
Sie kämen doch, nur wärens zwei
die furchtbar leise gingen. Dürfte er
sich einmal wenden (wäre das Zurückschaun
nicht die Zersetzung dieses ganzen Werkes,
das erst vollbracht wird), müßte er sie sehen,
die beiden Leisen, die ihm schweigend nachgehn:

Den Gott des Ganges und der weiten Botschaft,
die Reisehaube über hellen Augen,
den schlanken Stab hertragen vor dem Leibe
und flügelschlagend an den Fußgelenken;
und seiner linken Hand gegeben: *sie*.

And so they walked,

the wand of a man in an eye-blue cloak
hunted, intent, impatient to be there,
long ramshackle strides eating the thin path up,
arms uselessly hanging down his sides,
big lumps of fists protruding from the folds – no longer
conscious of the rose-delicate lyre
grafted to his forearm like a briar to an olive branch.
His senses bore the agony split minds undergo –
his sight out ahead, a hound on the scent,
now turning back at a bend to urge him on, now racing off
again; his hearing an odour already behind them,
faint, used. Maybe, he thought,
it even now reached back to them
and drew their footsteps on into his straining ear,
the two who were to ascend with him
through her heart… But it was only his own
steps echoing, the faint wind whipping his cloak.
Follow, follow – he heard it, heard
his own voice repeat it, his voice, his voice.
Their silence ate him up – how did they do it,
step so soundlessly and still follow?
He ached to understand, to know
them true to their words, to loose the hound
of his sight on them, to see – see
those grave two moving forward, silent but there –
yet knew if he turned now to look
he would look on tragedy… Those two –
a god – the Carrier of Distant Messages,
of inhuman speed, bright-eyed, dark-hooded,
wing-heeled, his staff pointing the way – and *she*.

Die So-geliebte, daß aus einer Leier
mehr Klage kam als je aus Klagefrauen;
daß eine Welt aus Klage ward, in der
alles noch einmal da war: Wald und Tal
und Weg und Ortschaft, Feld und Fluß und Tier;
und daß um diese Klage-Welt, ganz so
wie um die andre Erde, eine Sonne
und ein gestirnter stiller Himmel ging,
ein Klage-Himmel mit entstellten Sternen –:
Diese So-geliebte.

Sie aber ging an jenes Gottes Hand,
den Schritt beschränkt von langen Leichenbändern,
unsicher, sanft und ohne Ungeduld.
Sie war in sich, wie Eine hoher Hoffnung,
und dachte nicht des Mannes, der voranging,
und nicht des Weges, der ins Leben aufstieg.
Sie war in sich. Und ihr Gestorbensein
erfüllte sie wie Fülle.
Wie eine Frucht von Süßigkeit und Dunkel,
so war sie voll von ihrem großen Tode,
der also neu war, daß sie nichts begriff.

Sie war in einem neuen Mädchentum
und unberührbar; ihr Geschlecht war zu
wie eine junge Blume gegen Abend,
und ihre Hände waren der Vermählung
so sehr entwöhnt, daß selbst des leichten Gottes
unendlich leise, leitende Berührung
sie kränkte wie zu sehr Vertraulichkeit.

Sie war schon nicht mehr diese blonde Frau,
die in des Dichters Liedern manchmal anklang,
nicht mehr des breiten Bettes Duft und Eiland
und jenes Mannes Eigentum nicht mehr.

She – a woman so loved that a single lyre
untethered the lamentations leashed in every woman's throat
who ever lost a world. So loved
that mourning created and peopled a world
made of lament, with valleys and forests,
villages and teeming streams, animals and marketplaces;
a lament-world round which another sun travelled,
under a lament-heaven out of which anguished
stars stooped: a woman so loved.

She, embodying patience now, stilled
and inward-looking as a woman whose time has come,
her arm slipped through the god's, her gentle step
constrained by trailing tatters of shroud,
remained unconscious
of the upward-wending path they were treading,
and did not know the man, or the life readied for her in his world.
So inward was she, so filled with her death,
its sweetness – that of fruit already over – its darkness
spreading through her to the core; her death, too new,
too death-like; too all-encompassing to comprehend.

And new too was this cold virginity
which petrified her sex like a frosted flower.
It made the god's faint touch where his guiding arm
touched hers too much, as intimate almost
as an unsolicited kiss. For already

she was no man's property;
no longer the temptress with grey-blue eyes
whose name echoed through the poet's songs,
who answered him with the silks
and spicy sweetmeats of her body, who urged
him to take her again as a wave breaks over a beach…

Sie war schon aufgelöst wie langes Haar
und hingegeben wie gefallner Regen
und ausgeteilt wie hundertfacher Vorrat.

Sie war schon Wurzel.

Und als plötzlich jäh
der Gott sie anhielt und mit Schmerz im Ausruf
die Worte sprach: Er hat sich umgewendet –,
begriff sie nichts und sagte leise; *Wer?*

Fern aber, dunkel vor dem klaren Ausgang,
stand irgend jemand, dessen Angesicht
nicht zu erkennen war. Er stand und sah,
wie auf dem Streifen eines Wiesenpfades
mit trauervollem Blick der Gott der Botschaft
sich schweigend wandte, der Gestalt zu folgen,
die schon zurückging dieses selben Weges,
den Schritt beschränkt von langen Leichenbändern,
unsicher, sanft und ohne Ungeduld.

DER TURM

Tour St Nicholas, Furnes

Erd-Inneres. Als wäre dort, wohin
du blindlings steigst, erst Erdenoberfläche,
zu der du steigst im schrägen Bett der Bäche,
die langsam aus dem suchenden Gerinn

Already she was anyone's –
spreading herself like loosened hair,
common and prodigal as rain,
easily come by as corn, all men's currency.

She was nothing more than root…

So, when the god froze,
when suddenly, pitying them, he took hold of her lifeless hands
and told her *he has looked*, she, not understanding,
mouthed *who?*

The grieving god pointed with his staff. She saw,
vaguely, against the distant live world's sky,
the featureless silhouette of some man; who,
looking back down the winding sinew of path saw,
between dark meadows, that it entered her heart;
and that the God of Distant Messages had turned to follow –
for already she had turned
and was silently wending her way back down,
stilled and inward-looking, her gentle step
constrained by trailing tatters of shroud.

THE TOWER

Tour St Nicholas, Furnes

Buried. You must make a blind ascent
from the core to achieve the earth's surface,
push through drips and rivulets that strike your face
as they fall, then streams and torrents hellbent

der Dunkelheit entsprungen sind, durch die
sich dein Gesicht, wie auferstehend, drängt
und die du plötzlich *siehst*, als fiele sie
aus diesem Abgrund, der dich überhängt

und den du, wie er riesig über dir
sich umstürtzt in dem dämmernden Gestühle,
erkennst, erschreckt und fürchtend, im Gefühle:
o wenn er steigt, behangen wie ein Stier – :

Da aber nimmt dich aus der engen Endung
windiges Licht. Fast fliegend siehst du hier
die Himmel wieder, Blendung über Blendung,
und dort die Tiefen, wach und voll Verwendung,

und kleine Tage wie bei Patenier,
gleichzeitige, mit Stunde neben Stunde,
durch die die Brücken springen wie die Hunde,
dem hellen Wege immer auf der Spur,

den unbeholfne Häuser manchmal nur
verbergen, bis er ganz im Hintergrunde
beruhigt geht durch Buschwerk und Natur.

BEGEGNUNG IN DER KASTANIEN ALLEE

Ihm ward des Eingangs grüne Dunkelheit
kühl wie ein Seidenmantel umgegeben
den er noch nahm und ordnete: als eben
am andern transparenten Ende, weit,

on forcing you down as you fight up –
reaching for resurrection yet
soaked in the abyss – though glimpsing as you slip
on the slime-choked walls its massive fret-

work of ancient timbers, rotten, heavy, hanging
in the void over you, charged with the threat, all
the myth-inspiring musculature and posturing
potency of a ponderously-hung bull.

Then light – at last air and light pour
into your eyes and lungs as you prise
your body out of it and embrace
the skies as if you had wings and would soar

above the painter's landscape spreading
its pastel patchwork below, its taut
little leaping bridges chasing shadows like dogs,
past and present ribboned by one pale path, clogged

here with houses, there invitingly revealed,
as you pursue it to its vanishing point, lit
by the lowering sun, through copse and field.

ENCOUNTER IN THE CHESTNUT AVENUE

Entering that tunnel's green shade is
like feeling a silk garment settle on your skin.
Entering the far end where green radiance gleams in
as if through high uncertain stained glass

aus grüner Sonne, wie aus grünen Scheiben,
weiß eine einzelne Gestalt
aufleuchtete, um lange fern zu bleiben
und schließlich, von dem Lichterniedertreiben
bei jedem Schritte überwallt,

ein helles Wescheln auf sich herzutragen,
das scheu im Blond nach hinten lief.
Aber auf einmal war der Schatten tief,
und nahe Augen lagen aufgeschlagen

in einem neuen deutlichen Gesicht,
das wie einem Bildnis verweilte
in dem Moment, da man sich wieder teilte:
erst war es immer, und dann war es nicht.

O DIESES IST DAS TIER

O dieses ist das Tier, das es nicht giebt.
Sie wußtens nicht und habens jeden Falls
– sein Wandeln, seine Haltung, seinen Hals,
bis in des stillen Blickes Licht – geliebt.

Zwar *war* es nicht. Doch weil sie's liebten, ward
ein reines Tier. Sie ließen immer Raum.
Und in dem Raume, klar und ausgespart,
erhob es leicht sein Haupt und brauchte kaum

zu sein. Sie nährten es mit keinem Korn,
nur immer mit der Möglichkeit, es sei.
Und die gab solche Stärke an das Tier,

you catch, distant but seen, a certainty of shape,
a movement of white brilliance, a shining silhouette
in a drench of light, now seeming to approach, to step
nearer through the dazzle, now to stop –
and then again move deeper into your stare, to get

right into your pupils till it hurts to see,
glowing, pulsing closer, dissolving
into the shade then, suddenly lit again, becoming,
unforgettably, two eyes: then the exactly

delineated features of a face, caught
as if on camera in the instant of passing,
a snapshot of the unknown at the moment of meeting,
etched straight onto the retina then utterly wiped out.

O THIS IS THE ANIMAL THAT CANNOT BE

O this is the animal that cannot be,
never seen yet loved everywhere
for its movement, its poise, its arched neck, the clear
untroubled light in its eyes. How,

when it cannot be? To us who love it
it *is* there – pure, animal. We make space
for it and in that clear un-violated space
it can lightly raise its head without

needing to exist. We feed it, not on corn
but the simple possibilities
of being, which are so energising that some-

daß es aus sich ein Stirnhorn trieb. Ein Horn.
Zu einer Jungfrau kam es weiß herbei –
und war im Silber-Spiegel und in ihr.

DU, NIMMERGEKOMMENE

Du im Voraus
verlorne Geliebte, Nimmergekommene,
nicht weiß ich, welche Töne dir lieb sind.
Nicht mehr versuch ich, dich, wenn das Kommende wogt,
zu erkennen. Alle die großen
Bilder in mir, im Fernen erfahrene Landschaft,
Städte und Türme und Brücken und un-
vermutete Wendung der Wege
und das Gewaltige jener von Göttern
einst durchwachsenen Länder:
steigt zur Bedeutung in mir
deiner, Entgehende, an.

Ach, die Gärten bist du,
ach, ich sah sie mit solcher
Hoffnung. Ein offenes Fenster
im Landhaus – , und du tratest beinahe
mir nachdenklich heran. Gassen fand ich, –
du warst sie gerade gegangen,
und die Spiegel manchmal der Läden der Händler
waren noch schwindlich von dir und gaben erschrocken
mein zu plötzliches Bild. – Wer weiß, ob derselbe
Vogel nicht hinklang durch uns
gestern, einzeln, im Abend?

times a horn starts from its brow – one horn.
Ghost-pale, it haunts young girls, *is*
in their silver mirrors, *is* in them.

YOU, NEVER-ARRIVING ONE

You, never-arriving one, never-to-be-found sweetheart,
how can I know in advance
what songs will please you? Why go on
trying to recognize you in each moment's
surge of arrival? All the strongest
impressions I retain, the experience of distance's
landscapes, cities and towers and bridges, un-
suspected twists of the path
and that violence of the Gods
when they were creating these lands – all
take on their greatest significance in you;
and yet you still elude me.

Are these gardens not you?
I scan them with such hope! An open window
in a country lodge – and you, stepping out,
in a dwam, almost in front of me; streets
I wandered – you'd gone directly down them;
and sometimes shop mirrors, or market-traders',
still dizzy with you, were startled
by my too sudden image in them. Who knows whether
    the selfsame
bird didn't sound the alarm through us,
separately, yesterday evening?

LIEBES-LIED

Wie soll ich meine Seele halten, daß
sie nicht an deine rührt? Wie soll ich sie
hinheben über dich zu andern Dingen?
Ach gerne möcht ich sie bei irgendwas
verlorenem im Dunkel unterbringen
an einer fremdem stillen Stelle, die
nicht weiterschwingt, wenn deine Tiefen schwingen.
Doch alles, was uns anrührt, dich und mich,
nimmt uns zusammen wie ein Bogenstrich,
der aus zwei Saiten *eine* Stimme zieht.
Auf welches Instrument sind wir gespannt?
Und welcher Geiger hat uns in der Hand?
O süßes Lied.

DIE ENTFÜHRUNG

Oft war sie als Kind ihren Dienerinnen
entwichen, um die Nacht und den Wind
(weil sie drinnen so anders sind)
draußen zu sehn an ihrem Beginnen;
doch keine Sturmnacht hatte gewiß
den riesigen Park so in Stücke gerissen,
wie ihn jetzt ihr Gewissen zerriß,
da er sie nahm von der seidenen Leiter
und sie weitertrug, weiter, weiter…

bis der Wagen alles war.

LOVE SONG

Can my soul be prevented from touching yours?
How? How can I lift it beyond yours
to the stars, and higher? If I could hide my soul from yours
in the wall-less wardrobe of space, free it in time from yours,
let it spin with dark lost things and not tremble when yours
calls out to it… ah, but how my soul seeks yours…

Whatever touches *yours* or *mine* is *ours*.
Doesn't the violin's bow spanning two souls like ours
draw out a richer note, two joys as one – ours?
Whose instrument are we strung so tautly across? Ours.
Whose are the sensitive hands that cradle it? Ours.
And whose the tongues teasing song from its neck and sweet
    belly? Ours –
the song is ours!

THE ABDUCTION

Because she must feel… So often as a child
she absconded into the night, where exposed to every element
she learned through her skin how different
a nursery's breathings are from the wild's.
Child, tonight it is the storm of your conscience
which shreds the air as you descend the silken rungs
into his arms; which carry you – as the wind's insistence
bundles leaf-clouds through the park – further
and further until you are delivered

into the carriage; which, suddenly, is all.

Und sie roch inn, den schwarzen Wagen,
um den verhalten das Jagen stand
und die Gefahr.
Und sie fand ihn mit Kaltem ausgeschlagen;
und das Schwarze and Kalte war auch in ihr.
Sie kroch in ihren Mantelkragen
und befühlte ihr Haar, als bliebe es hier,
und hörte fremd einen Fremden sagen:
Ichbinbeidir.

LEDA

Als ihn der Gott in seiner Not betrat,
erschrak er fast, den Schwan so schön zu finden;
er ließ sich ganz verwirrt in ihm verschwinden.
Schon aber trug ihn sein Betrug zur Tat,

bevor er noch des unerprobten Seins
Gefühle prüfte. Und die Aufgetane
erkannte schon den Kommenden im Schwane
und wußte schon: er bat um Eins,

das sie, verwirrt in ihrem Widerstand,
nicht mehr verbergen konnte. Er kam nieder
und halsend durch die immer schwächre Hand

ließ sich der Gott in die Geliebte los.
Dann erst empfand er glücklich sein Gefieder
und wurde wirklich Schwan in ihrem Schooß.

O the reek of danger
in that black carriage, of passion and pursuit –
even its dank upholstery fills
you with ravenous feeling – as if a stranger
had buried her face in a stranger's greatcoat collar
and he were caressing her hair – her golden gift to him –
and whispered in his throat to her,
blurted it meaninglessly as if his lips were numb,
I'mwithyouhere.

LEDA

Then the passion-driven God transforms
himself. He hides in the swan, but finds
his heart overawed by its beauty; nor does he understand
the marvel of being *swan* as he storms

towards his desire. Entranced, she sees
within the snowy form the God's advance,
knows what he lusts for. She moans 'no' once
then a blow from his white-quilled wing topples

her – the coil of the neck snakes out of her hand,
he loosens her thighs and opening her thrusts in
– O deep delight – drives deep, dissolves… This was the
    purposed end

of their strife – this God-swan, as he convulses
in her undone flesh, truly becoming swan;
preening his swan-feathers in her eyes.

ABSCHIED

Wie hab ich das gefühlt was Abschied heißt.
Wie weiß ichs noch: ein dunkles unverwundnes
grausames Etwas, das ein Schönverbundnes
noch einmal zeigt und hinhält und zerreißt.

Wie war ich ohne Wehr, dem zuzuschauen,
das, da es mich, mich rufend, gehen ließ,
zurückblieb, so als wärens alle Frauen
und dennoch klein und weiß und nichts als dies:

Ein Winken, schon nicht mehr auf mich bezogen,
ein leise Weiterwinkendes – , schon kaum
erklärbar mehr: vielleicht ein Pflaumenbaum,
von dem ein Kuckuck hastig abgeflogen.

DIE GENESENDE

Wie ein Singen kommt und geht in Gassen
und sich nähert und sich wieder scheut,
flügelschlagend, manchmal fast zu fassen
und dann wieder weit hinausgestreut:

spielt mit der Genesenden das Leben;
während sie, geschwächt und ausgeruht,
unbeholfen, um sich hinzugeben,
eine ungewohnte Geste tut.

Und sie fühlt es beinah wie Verführung,
wenn die hartgewordne Hand, darin
Fieber waren voller Widersinn,
fernher, wie mit blühender Berührung,
zu liebkosen kommt ihr hartes Kinn.

PARTING

Never let the shape we make be that of parting –
it has the look and feel of implacable cruelty.
Who made the world this way? Why
offer the fruit up whole then pulp it? Nothing

describes the raw thing I became when she
clutched me closer in order to let me go –
so that she might remain, she cried, stay
in her pale woman-form to wave goodbye,

goodbye, though no longer, it seemed, to me,
so slight and inward was her waving.
Years on, in my heart, leaves fluttering
as if a cuckoo had just flown from the damson-tree.

THE CONVALESCENT

It's like singing half-heard in the street;
you seem to hear it, and then you don't;
from the sibilant vibrato of a lark's ascent
to a moth's wing-beat –

so life flirts with the weak.
And she – drained, convalescing –
can only summon up one trick
in reply; but her hand – dry, gesturing,

feverishly grasping at the insubstantial,
there but not here, far off
but awakened to sensation, cannot reach – as if
a too shy seducer keeps trying but fails
to caress her fevered cheek.

CHRISTI HÖLLENFAHRT

Endlich verlitten, entging sein Wesen dem schrecklichen
Leibe der Leiden. Oben. Ließ ihn.
Und die Finsternis fürchtete sich allein
und warf an das Bleiche
Fledermäuse heran, – immer noch schwankt abends
in ihrem Flattern die Angst vor dem Anprall
an die erkaltete Qual. Dunkle ruhlose Luft
entmutigte sich an dem Leichnam; und in den starken
wachsamen Tieren der Nacht war Dumpfheit und Unlust.
Sein entlassener Geist gedachte vielleicht in der Landschaft
anzustehen, unhandelnd. Denn seiner Leidung Ereignis
war noch genug. Maßvoll
schien ihm der Dinge nächtliches Dastehn,
und wie ein trauriger Raum griff er darüber um sich.
Aber die Erde, vertrocknet im Durst seiner Wunden,
aber die Erde riß auf, und es rufte im Abgrund.
Er, Kenner der Martern, hörte die Hölle
herheulend, begehrend Bewußtsein
seiner vollendeten Not: daß über dem Ende der seinen
(unendlichen) ihre, währende Pein erschrecke, ahne.
Und er stürzte, der Geist, mit der völligen Schwere
seiner Erschöpfung herein: schritt als ein Eilender
durch das befremdete Nachschaun weidender Schatten,
hob zu Adam den Aufblick, eilig,
eilte hinab, schwand, schien und verging in dem Stürzen
wilderer Tiefen. Plötzlich (höher, höher) über der Mitte
aufschäumender Schreie, auf dem langen
Turm seines Duldens trat er hervor: ohne Atem,
stand, ohne Geländer, Eigentümer der Schmerzen. Schwieg.

CHRIST'S DESCENT INTO HELL

Past temptation at last, his soul escaped the terrible
body of suffering. Above. Gone from him.
And the darkness was afraid of being alone,
and flung bats against the wan light –
in whose flutterings tremulous evenings
expressed their fear of making contact with that
chilling agony. The dim changeable air
lost confidence in itself before the corpse, even
strong alert night-animals grew vague and listless.
Perhaps his redundant spirit hoped to linger on
in that landscape, passively; what had happened –
his Agony – was still enough. This night-time
standing-there of Things seemed disengaging to him,
he might grope his way about like some sad space.
But the earth, drained dry by his thirsting wounds –
but the earth, it split open and something cried out from the abyss.
He, connoisseur of torture, heard Hell howling,
desperate for understanding of his perfected need;
that through the medium of his (unending) anguish it
might get the measure of its own perpetual pain.
Weighed down by his exhaustion his spirit plunged
into it, strode like a hurrying man, passed the astonished stares
of grazing shades, glanced hurriedly up
at Adam, hurried down, down, vanished,
gleamed as, hurtling down, he passed
into wilder depths. Suddenly (higher, higher), up above
the core of up-foaming screams, he stepped out
onto his tall tower of suffering, stood there without
breathing, with no support-rail, proprietor of all pain. Silent.

DUISENER ELEGIEN: DIE ERSTE ELEGIE

Wer, wenn ich schriee, hörte mich denn aus der Engel
Ordnungen? Und gesetzt selbst, es nähme
einer mich plötzlich ans Herz: ich verginge von seinem
stärkeren Dasein. Denn das Schöne ist nichts
als des schrecklichen Anfang, den wir noch grade ertragen,
und wir bewundern es so, weil es gelassen verschmäht,
uns zu zerstören. Ein jeder Engel ist schrecklich.
    Und so verhalt ich mich denn und verschlucke den Lockruf
dunkeln Schluchzens. Ach, wen vermögen
wir denn zu brauchen? Engel nicht, Menschen nicht,
und die findigen Tiere merken es schon,
daß wir nicht sehr verläßlich zu Haus sind
in der gedeuteten Welt. Es bleibt uns vielleicht
irgend ein Baum an dem Abhang, daß wir ihn täglich
wiedersähen; es bleibt uns die Straße von gestern
und das verzogene Treusein einer Gewohnheit,
der es bei uns gefiel, und so blieb sie und ging nicht.
    O und die Nacht, die Nacht, wenn der Wind voller Weltraum
uns am Angesicht zehrt –, wem bliebe sie nicht, die ersehnte,
sanft enttäuschende, welche dem einzelnen Herzen
mühsam bevorsteht. Ist sie den Liebenden leichter?
Ach, sie verdecken sich nur mit einander ihr Los.
    Weißt du's *noch* nicht? Wirf aus den Armen die Leere
zu den Räumen hinzu, die wir atmen; vielleicht daß die Vögel
die erweiterte Luft fühlen mit innigerm Flug.

Ja, die Frühlinge brauchten dich wohl. Es muteten manche
Sterne dir zu, daß du sie spürtest. Es hob
sich eine Woge heran im Vergangenen, oder
da du vorüberkamst am geöffneten Fenster,
gab eine Geige sich hin. Das alles war Auftrag.
Aber bewältigtest du's? Warst du nicht immer
noch von Erwartung zerstreut, als kündigte alles
eine Geliebte dir an? (Wo willst du sie bergen,

DUINO ELEGIES: FIRST ELEGY

If I cried out, who amongst the angels' hierarchies
would hear me? Suppose one of them suddenly
pressed me to his heart; I would be crushed
by his more forceful existence. For beauty is nothing
but the onset of terror – which we can still just bear,
and which we so admire, because it so serenely deigns
not to destroy us. All angels prove terrifying.
     And so I restrain myself, and swallow my dark sobs'
calls – ah, who is there for us
when we need them? Not angels, not men,
and the prescient animals have already observed
that we are uneasily at home
in our interpreted world. Perhaps all that remains
for us is some tree on a slope, one we can re-imagine
day after day; or yesterday's street remains, having
the tenacity of a habit which becomes so entrenched
when we adopt it that it stays, will never leave.
     Oh and there is night, there are nights filled
with cosmic winds which erode our faces.
Whom will she not wait for, that longed-for
quietly disappointing one in whom the solitary's heart-
sorrows grow? Is it easier for lovers? No,
their loving conceals what's inevitable in each other.
     Do you *still* not understand? Hurl this emptiness out of your arms
into the spaces we breathe. Perhaps the birds
will sense how the air is added to, and fly it more passionately.

Yes; sometimes springtime needs you. Many a time
stars lingered, wanting to feel through you. Many
a wave rolls out of history towards you, or,
as you pass an open window, some violin
will be giving its utmost. All this was assigned –
but are you equal to it? Aren't you always
on tenterhooks, as if every event anticipates
a lover's arrival? (How will you contain her

da doch die großen fremden Gedanken bei dir
aus und ein gehn und öfters bleiben bei Nacht).
Sehnt es dich aber, so singe die Liebenden; lange
noch nicht unsterblich genug ist ihr berühmtes Gefühl.
Jene, du neidest sie fast, Verlassenen, die du
so viel liebender fandst als die Gestillten. Beginn
immer von neuem die nie zu erreichende Preisung;
denk: es erhält sich der Held, selbst der Untergang war ihm
nur ein Vorwand, zu sein: seine letzte Geburt.
Aber die Liebenden nimmt die erschöpfte Natur
In sich zurück, als wären nicht zweimal die Kräfte,
dieses zu leisten. Hast du der Gaspara Stampa
den genügend gedacht, daß irgend ein Mädchen,
dem der Geliebte entging, am gesteigerten Beispiel
dieser Liebenden fühlt: daß ich würde wie sie?
Sollen nicht endlich uns diese ältesten Schmerzen
fruchtbarer werden? Ist es nicht Zeit, daß wir liebend
uns vom Geliebten befrein und es bebend bestehn:
wie der Pfeil die Sehne besteht, um gesammelt im Absprung
mehr zu sein als er selbst. Denn Bleiben ist nirends.

Stimmen. Stimmen. Höre, mein Herz, wie sonst nur
Heilige hörten: daß sie der riesige Ruf
aufhob vom Boden; sie aber knieten,
Unmögliche, weiter und achtetens nicht:
So waren sie hörend. Nicht, daß du *Gottes* ertrügest
die Stimme, bei weitem. Aber das Wehende höre,
die ununterbrochene Nachricht, die aus Stille sich bildet.
Es rauscht jetzt von jenen jungen Toten zu dir.
Wo immer du eintratst, redete nicht in Kirchen
zu Rom and Neapel ruhig ihr Schicksal dich an?
Oder es trug eine Inschrift sich erhaben dir auf,
wie neulich die Tafel in Santa Maria Formosa.
Was sie mir wollen? leise soll ich des Unrechts

while all those strange great coming and going
thoughts inhabit your nights!).
But if you yearn, sing those who love;
for that legendary emotion is still not immortal enough.
Sing the most rejected – whom you almost envy –
whom you find you can love so much more than the satisfied.
Begin, and again begin, the unattainable praising;
consider – the hero survives, even his decline
is just a pretext for living on, his latest birth.
While Nature, exhausted, re-absorbs lovers
as if lacking the strength to create them twice over.
Is Gaspara Stampa sufficiently etched on the modern mind,
so that any girl abandoned by her lover might feel
the soaring example of her loving and cry let me be her!
Shouldn't this ancient pain bear fruit for us now?
Has the time not come for us lovingly
to free our lovers, and, tremblingly, to endure?
As the arrow endures the longed-for bow-string
so that in the pent-up spasm of release
it can be more than itself? For to remain is to be nowhere.

Voices. Voices. Hear them, my heart,
as the saints must have heard them; who were lifted
from the ground by their vast calling – though still
kneeling, impossibly, without knowing it was happening, so
utter was their hearing. We are far
from being able to bear the voice of God, but listen
to the nascent message that ceaselessly forms itself from silence.
Its whisperings reach you now from those who died too young –
didn't their fates quietly importune you
whenever you entered a church in Naples or Rome?
Or when an inscription exalted you with its meaning,
as, recently, on that tablet in Santa Maria Formosa?
What do they want of me? That I should gently

Anschein abtun, der ihrer Geister
reine Bewegung manchmal ein wenig behindert.

Freilich ist es seltsam, die Erde nicht mehr zu bewohnen,
kaum erlernte Gebräuche nicht mehr zu üben,
Rosen, und andern eigens versprechenden Dingen
nicht die Bedeutung menschlicher Zukunft zu geben;
das, was man war in unendlich ängstlichen Händen,
nicht mehr zu sein, und selbst den eigenen Namen
wegzulassen wie ein zerbrochenes Spielzeug.
Seltsam, die Wünsche nicht weiterzuwünschen. Seltsam,
alles, was sich bezog, so lose im Raume
flattern zu sehen. Und das Totsein ist mühsam
und voller Nachholn, daß man allmählich ein wenig
Ewigkeit spürt. – Aber Lebendige machen
alle den Fehler, daß sie zu stark unterscheiden.
Engel (sagt man) wüßten oft nicht, ob sie unter
Lebenden gehn oder Toten. Die ewige Strömung
reißt durch beide Bereiche alle Alter
immer mit sich übertönt sie in beiden.

Schließlich brauchen sie uns nicht mehr, die Früheentrückten,
man entwöhnt sich des Irdischen sanft, wie man den Brüsten
milde der Mutter entwächst. Aber wir, die so große
Geheimnisse brauchen, denen aus Trauer so oft
seliger Fortschritt entspringt – : *könnten* wir sein ohne sie?
Ist die Sage umsonst, daß einst in der Klage um Linos
wagende erste Musik dürre Erstarrung durchdrang;
daß erst im erschrockenen Raum, dem ein beinah göttlicher Jüngling
    Jüngling
plötzlich für immer enttrat, das Leere in jene
Schwingung geriet, die uns jetzt hinreißt und tröstet und hilft.

counter the appearance of wrong, which sometimes
subtly impedes their spirits' pure movement.

Admittedly it is strange no longer to inhabit this earth,
no longer to use scarcely-learned customs,
not to give roses, and other Things which promise
so much, their meanings, a human future;
no longer to be all one was
in endlessly anxious hands; even to dispose of
one's own first name like some broken toy.
Strange, not to desire our desires. Strange
to see all which was related let loose,
set fluttering in space. And being dead
is arduous, filled with gathering yourself
before you can gradually experience a little eternity.
But the living all make the mistake of too
sharply distinguishing – isn't it said that angels
can barely tell whether they move amongst
the living or the dead? The eternal tide
forever sweeps the ages along with it through both great realms,
and both are drowned in its thunder.

At last the too-early-taken no longer need us.
They are weaned from the Earthly as gently as children
outgrowing their mothers' soft breasts. But we, who so utterly
need the great Mysteries, we, who so frequently find grief
is the source of our spirits' growth – without them can we be?
Does Linus' story no longer signify, in which
we are told how the first bold song-notes pierced the parched
    numbness,
how in startled space, suddenly abandoned forever by the
    godlike youth,
Nowhereness first thrilled to that vibration
which lifts up and comforts and enraptures us still.

AM RANDE DER NACHT

Meine Stube und diese Weite,
wach über nachtendem Land, –
ist Eines. Ich bin eine Saite,
über rauschende breite
Resonanzen gespannt.

Die Dinge sind Geigenleiber,
von murrendem Dunkel voll;
drin träumt das Weinen der Weiber,
drin rührt sich im Schlafe der Groll
ganzer Geschlechter…
Ich soll
silbern erzittern: dann wird
Alles unter mir leben,
und was in den Dingen irrt,
wird nach dem Lichte streben,
das von meinem tanzenden Tone,
um welchen der Himmel wellt,
durch schmale, schmachtende Spalten
in die alten
Abgründe ohne
Ende fällt…

AN DIE MUSIK

Musik: Atem der Statuen. Vielleicht:
Stille der Bilder. Du Sprache wo Sprachen
enden. Du Zeit,
die senkrecht steht auf der Richtung vergehender Herzen.

ON THE VERGE OF NIGHT

My room, and space watching
over the land's dark distances –
are one. I am a string
stretched taut across the far-reaching
thundering resonances.

Things are violin-bodies
full of reverberating darkness –
in it dream the cries
of women, in its sleep the bitterness
of whole generations is roused…
I'll thrum, luminous
as silver. Then all
that is beneath me will come alive,
and whatever struggles
to find its way in Things will strive
towards the brightness
which from my dancing tone –
around which skies pulsate –
endlessly falls through fissures, thin
and disconsolate,
to the ancient abyss…

TO MUSIC

Music. Breath of statues. Perhaps;
stillness's image. You language
beyond language. You Time
standing perpendicular to the trajectory of our hearts.

Gefühle zu wem? O du der Gefühle
Wandlung in was?… In hörbare Landschaft.
Du Fremde: Musik. Du uns entwachsener
Herzraum. Innigstes unser,
das, uns übersteigend, hinausdrängt, –
heiliger Abschied:
da uns das Innre umsteht
als geübteste Ferne, als andre
Seite der Luft:
rein,
riesig,
nicht mehr bewohnbar.

GONG

Nicht mehr für Ohren… Klang,
der, wie ein tieferes Ohr,
uns, scheinbar Hörende, hört.
Umkehr der Räume. Entwurf
innerer Welten in Frein…
Tempel vor ihrer Geburt,
Lösung, gesättigt mit schwer
löslichen Göttern… Gong!

Summe des Schweigenden, das
sich zu sich selber bekennt,
brausende Einkehr in sich
dessen, das an sich verstummt,
Dauer, aus Ablauf gepreßt,
um-gegossener Stern… Gong!

Feeling – for whom? O you who are feeling
transformed into… what?… Audible landscape!
You stranger; music. You who have outgrown
our heartspace. Our innermost selves
which, surpassing us, break out of us –
sacred departure.
When what is most deeply us
exists out there as our most experienced distance, as the other
side of the air;
pure,
vast,
uninhabitable.

GONG

Beyond all hearing… Boom!
Like a deeper ear hearing
us, its would-be hearers.
Space turned inside out. Our innermost
worlds outlined in the air…
A temple before her birth, now
solution sated with no-longer soluble
gods… Gong!

Culmination of silences,
acknowledging only itself, taking
all that is thunderous into itself
from what it has struck dumb.
Permanence wrung from what passes,
newly-poured star… Gong!

Du, die man niemals vergißt,
die sich gebar in Verlust,
nichtmer begriffenes Fest,
Wein an unsichtbarem Mund,
Sturm in der Säule, die trägt,
Wanderers Sturz in der Weg,
unser, an Alles, Verrat… Gong!

EIN GOTT VERMAGS. WIE ABER, SAG MIR, SOLL

Ein Gott vermags. Wie aber, sag mir, soll
ein Mann ihm folgen durch die schmale Leier?
Sein Sinn ist Zwiespalt. An der Kreuzung zweier
Herzwege steht kein Tempel für Apoll.

Gesang, wie du ihn lehrst, ist nicht Begehr,
nicht Werbung um ein endlich noch Erreichtes;
Gesang ist Dasein. Für den Gott ein Leichtes.
Wann aber *sind* wir? Und wann endet *er*

An unser Sein die Erde und die Sterne?
Dies *ists* nicht, Jüngling, daß du liebst, wenn auch
die Stimme dann den Mund dir aufstößt, – lerne

vergessen, daß du aufsangst. Das verrinnt.
In Wahrheit singen, ist ein andrer Hauch.
Ein Hauch um nichts. Ein Wehn im Gott. Ein Wind.

You, who are unforgettable,
casualty of your own birth –
who can no more embrace celebration –
are wine on invisible lips,
storm in the stoic's pillar,
the wanderer's fall by the wayside,
betrayer of every Thing… Gong!

A GOD CAN DO IT, BUT YOU TELL ME HOW

A god can do it – but you tell me how
a man can follow him through the fine-strung lyre!
Our minds are divided. In our hearts, where
life's roads cross, stand no temples to Apollo.

You taught us that song is not desire, it
does not aspire to consummation.
Song is existence. Simple for a god but when
are we? Tell us, when *shall* we inherit

the earth and stars? Young ones, it is not
that you love, even though love's voice
has forced your mouths wide open – learn to forget

those involuntary songs; they will end.
True singing's a different breath. It has no choice,
being nothing. A tremor in a god. A wind.

DER EINSAME

Wie einer, der auf fremden Meeren fuhr,
so bin ich bei den ewig Einheimischen;
die vollen Tage stehn auf ihren Tischen,
mir aber ist die Ferne voll Figur.

In mein Gesicht reicht eine Welt herein,
die vielleicht unbewohnt ist wie ein Mond,
sie aber lassen kein Gefühl allein,
und alle ihre Worte sind bewohnt.

Die Dinge, die ich weither mit mir nahm,
sehn selten aus, gehalten an das Ihre – ;
in ihrer großen Heimat sind die Tiere,
hier halten sie den Atem an vor Scham.

DU SIEHST, ICH WILL VIEL

Du siehst, ich will viel.
Vielleicht will ich Alles:
das Dunkel jedes unendlichen Falles
und jedes Steigens lichtzitterndes Spiel.

Es leben so viele und wollen nichts,
und sind durch ihres leichten Gerichts
glatte Gefühle gefürstet.

Aber du freust dich jedes Gesichts,
das dient und dürstet.

Du freust dich Aller, die dich gebrauchen
wie ein Gerät.

THE SOLITARY

As someone crossing an unknown sea –
that's how I am among these locals.
Days might complete themselves round their tables
but it's distance that transfigures me.

Another world illuminates my face,
which seems, perhaps, deserted as the moon;
but these daren't risk one feeling out of place,
or hear any words but their own.

Looked at seldom, not held in high esteem,
are the Things I brought from far off.
In their own great country they strode bold as life,
but here they hold their breath for shame.

YOU SEE, I WANT A LOT

You see, I want a lot.
Perhaps I want it all –
the dark's unstoppable fall,
the rise and dapple of light.

So many fail to ask, choose
their surface emotions, refuse
to aspire. Aren't you

gladdened by every face
which thirsts and serves? Aren't you

gladdened when humankind
uses you as a tool?

Noch bist du nicht kalt, und es ist nicht zu spät,
In deine werdenden Tiefen zu tauchen,
wo sich das Leben ruhig verrät.

BILDNIS

Daß von dem verzichtenden Gesichte
keiner ihrer großen Schmerzen fiele,
trägt sie langsam durch die Trauerspiele
ihrer Züge schönen welken Strauß,
wild gebunden und schon beinah lose;
manchmal fällt, wie eine Tuberose,
ein verlornes Lächeln müd heraus.

Und sie geht gelassen drüber hin,
müde, mit den schönen blinden Händen,
welche wissen, daß sie es nicht fänden, –

und sie sagt Erdichtetes, darin
Schicksal schwankt, gewolltes, irgendeines,
und sie giebt ihm ihrer Seele Sinn,
daß es ausbricht wie ein Ungemeines:
wie das Schreien eines Steines –

und sie läßt, mit hochgehobnem Kinn,
alle diese Worte wieder fallen,
ohne bleibend; denn nicht eins von allen
ist der wehen Wirklichkeit gemaß,
ihrem einzigen Eigentum,
das sie, wie ein fußloses Gefäß,
halten muß, hoch über ihren Ruhm
und der Gang der Abende hinaus.

You aren't yet cold, there's time still
to plunge to the deepening depths of your mind
where life quietly unveils.

PORTRAIT

Must she wear her private woes
on her public face? So she denies them,
makes a faded posy of her features. *Come,*
she says, lifting that fatigued bouquet,
life will unravel secrets beyond these tragedies;
and a small smile drops like a tuberose
from her lips, wearily.

She steps indifferently round it
knowing the beautiful hands
she extends out of her weariness are blind

to it. Like us she fabricates
lovely meaningless meanings from her soul's
uniqueness, the utter ordinariness of its fate;
which is to smile
at breaking waves whilst screaming like a pebble.

Any word she might have spoken she lets
fall, her proud face lifted, for what have words
to do with the raw world she accords
the name *reality,* her one possession?
She carries it with her, the vase of it
held high above her head like a trophy, a distinction
she can't disown, must bear its weight
alone in the evenings' procession.

DUINESER ELEGIEN: DIE VIERTE ELEGIE

O Bäume Lebens, o wann winterlich?
Wir sind nicht einig. Sind nicht wie die Zug-
vögel verständigt. Überholt und spät,
so drängen wir uns plötzlich Winden auf
und fallen ein auf teilnahmslosen Teich.
Blühn und verdorrn ist uns zugleich bewußt.
Und irgendwo gehn Löwen noch und wissen,
solang sie herrlich sind, von keiner Ohnmacht.

Uns aber, wo wir eines meinen, ganz,
ist schon des andern Aufwand fühlbar. Feindschaft
ist uns das Nächste. Treten Liebende
nicht immerfort an Ränder, eins im andern,
die sich versprachen Weite, Jagd und Heimat.
    Da wird für eines Augenblickes Zeichnung
ein Grund von Gegenteil bereitet, müsham,
daß wir sie sähen; denn man ist sehr deutlich
mit uns. Wir kennen den Kontur
des Fühlens nicht: nur, was ihn formt von außen.
    Wer saß nicht bang vor seines Herzens Vorhang?
Der schlug sich auf: die Szenerie war Abschied.
Leicht zu verstehen. Der bekannte Garten,
und schwankte leise: dann erst kam der Tänzer.
Nicht *der*. Genug! Und wenn er auch so leicht tut,
er ist verkleidet und er wird ein Bürger
und geht durch seine Küche in die Wohnung.
    Ich will nicht diese halbgefüllten Masken,
lieber die Puppe. Die ist voll. Ich will
den Balg aushalten und den Draht und ihr
Gesicht aus Aussehn. Hier. Ich bin davor.
Wenn auch die Lampen ausgehn, wenn mir auch
gesagt wird: Nichts mehr – , wenn auch von Bühne
das Leere herkommt mit dem grauen Luftzug,
wenn auch von meinen stillen Vorfahrn keiner
mehr mit mir dasitzt, keine Frau, sogar

DUINO ELEGIES: THE FOURTH ELEGY

O trees of life, when is our winter?
We are not attuned, are not instinctively aware
like migratory birds. Far too late
we suddenly urge ourselves out into the wind,
only to fall beside some torpid pond.
We simultaneously flower and fade;
yet somewhere lions still prowl who in their majesty
cannot imagine such frailty.

But we, absorbed in one thing, are already
weighing the impact of another. Conflict
grows naturally in us. Don't lovers
continually come up against each others' limitations,
despite their promises of openness, shared work and home?
    Even for a cursory sketch a contrasting
background is laid down, with care,
against which we can more distinctly see –
for we never know the contours of our own feelings,
only the external factors which form them.
    Who does not sit, afraid, before his heart's
curtain? It jolts up: the scenery of parting.
Simple to understand: that familiar garden,
slightly swaying, then the dancer coming on –
not *him*! Enough! No matter how supple his movements
he's just a bourgeois in costume – he'll walk in through
the kitchen when he arrives home.
    I won't accept these half-stuffed masks –
a puppet would be preferable, it's full. I'll
tolerate the doll worked by wires, and its face
which is only appearance. Here. I'm waiting.
Even if the lights are extinguished; even if someone
whispers "it's over". Even if emptiness
enters me in a grey draught from the stage,
even if my silent ancestors no longer
sit with me, not even one woman, no longer

der Knabe nicht mehr mit dem braunen Schielaug:
Ich bleibe dennoch. Es giebt immer Zuschaun.

Hab ich nicht recht? Du, der um mich so bitter
das Leben schmeckte, meines kostend, Vater,
den ersten trüben Aufguß meines Müssens,
da ich heranwuchs, immer wieder kostend
und, mit dem Nachgeschmack so fremder Zukunft
beschäftigt, prüftest mein beschlagnes Aufschaun, –
der du, mein Vater, seit du tot bist, oft
in meiner Hoffnung, innen in mir, Angst hast,
und Gleichmut, wie ihn Tote haben, Reiche
von Gleichmut, aufgiebst für mein bißchen Schicksal,
hab ich nicht recht? Und ihr, hab ich nicht recht,
die ihr mich liebtet für den kleinen Anfang
Liebe zu euch, von dem ich immer abkam,
weil mir der Raum in eurem Angesicht,
da ich ihn liebte, überging in Weltraum,
in dem ihr nicht mehr wart…: wenn mir zumut ist,
zu warten vor der Puppenbühne, nein,
so völlig hinzuschaun, daß, um mein Schauen
am Ende aufzuwiegen, dort als Spieler
ein Engel hinmuß, der die Bälge hochreißt.
Engel und Puppe: dann ist endlich Schauspiel.
Dann kommt zusammen, was wir immerfort
entzwein, indem wir da sind. Dann entsteht
aus unsern Jahreszeiten erst der Umkreis
des ganzen Wandelns. Über uns hinüber
spielt dann der Engel. Sieh, die Sterbenden,
sollten sie nicht vermuten, wie voll Vorwand
das alles ist, was wir hier leisten. Alles
ist nicht es selbst. O Stunden in der Kindheit,
da hinter den Figuren mehr als nur
Vergangnes war und vor uns nicht die Zukunft.
Wir wuchsen freilich und wir drängten manchmal,

even that brown-eyed boy with the squint –
I'll sit it out anyway. One can always spectate.

I'm right, aren't I? You, father, for whom the flavour
of life turned bitter after you tasted mine –
that first inordinate outpouring of balked will ;
who as I grew up must continually taste
and, preoccupied by the after-taste of so strange
a future, try to fathom my too obscure gazing.
You, my father, who since you died have so often
feared for me, and my most intimate hopes,
and relinquished that serenity the dead achieve,
whole realms of equanimity, for my little fate –
I'm right, aren't I? And you – aren't I right? – you
women who loved me because of my hesitant beginnings
of love for you, which I always retreated from
because the universe of your features, which I loved,
expanded to a cosmos in which you
no longer existed. Is it not reasonable of me
to wait in front of the puppet-booth – or rather
to so utterly out-stare it that to counteract
my stare an angel must play his part
in goading the doll into life? Angel
and puppet; now that would be a show!
Then there would be joined what we, simply by
being, always part. Only then will change arise
from the cycle of our seasons. Then, above us,
all around us, the angel will play. Look, you dying
who are not meant to notice, how full of dissembling
all our achievements in this life are. Nothing
is what it would be. O childhood hours,
when behind your figures stood something more than the past
and what stretched before us was not our future.
We grew strongly, were sometimes impatient

bald groß zu werden, denen halb zulieb,
die andres nicht mehr hatten, als das Großsein.
Und waren doch, in unserem Alleingehn,
mit Dauerndem vergnügt und standen da
im Zwischenraume zwischen Welt und Spielzeug,
an einer Stelle, die seit Anbeginn
gegründet war für einen reinen Vorgang.

Wer zeigt ein Kind, so wie es steht? Wer stellt
es ins Gestirn und giebt das Maß des Abstands
ihm in die Hand? Wer macht den Kindertod
aus grauem Brot, das hart wird, – oder läßt
ihn drin im runden Mund, so wie den Gröps
von einem schönen Apfel?… Mörder sind
leicht einzusehen. Aber dies: den Tod,
den ganzen Tod, noch *vor* dem Leben so
sanft zu enthalten und nicht bös zu sein,
ist unbeschreiblich.

IRRE IM GARTEN

Dijon

Noch schließt die aufgegebene Kartause
sich um den Hof, als würde etwas heil.
Auch die sie jetzt bewohnen, haben Pause
und nehmen nicht am Leben draußen teil.

Was irgend kommen konnte, das verlief.
Nun gehn sie gerne mit bekannten Wegen,
und trennen sich und kommen sich entgegen,
als ob sie kreisten, willig, primitiv.

to be grown-up too, half in order to please
those others who had nothing more, only their grown-up-ness;
most childlike when playing by ourselves
with timeless joy in that gap
between the real and unreal, the world and toys,
a place which from the very first
was saved for such innocent happenings…

Who truly depicts a child?
Who locates him amongst the stars, and places
the instruments of measurement in his hand? Who
makes him a child-sized Death from grey bread, which hardens,
or lies like a sweet apple's awkward core
in the round of his mouth? To murder
is understandable – but this; that we can so tenderly
cradle our deaths, the whole of death, even before
we are born and yet still embrace life,
is inexpressible.

THE ASYLUM GARDEN

Dijon

The courtyard is still enclosed
by cloisters and cells; is still a healing place;
but home now to others who've also refused
the world, who also were constrained to choose

what happens within themselves, not life.
When many travel one familiar path,
diverging here, converging there, never outwith
one simple unchanging circle, each finds relief;

Zwar manche pflegen dort die Frühlingsbeete,
demütig, dürftig, hingekniet;
aber sie haben, wenn es keiner sieht,
eine verheimlichte, verdrehte

Gebärde für das zarte frühe Gras,
ein prüfendes, verschüschtertes Liebkosen:
denn das ist freundlich, und das Rot der Rosen
wird vielleicht drohend sein und Übermaß

und wird vielleicht schon wieder übersteigen,
was ihre Seele wiederkennt und weiß.
Dies aber läßt sich noch verschweigen:
wie gut das Gras ist und wie leis.

SIEHE DIE BLUMEN, DIESE DEM IRDISCHEN TREUEN

Siehe die Blumen, diese dem Irdischen treuen,
denen wir Schicksal vom Rande des Schicksals leihn, –
aber wer weiß es! Wenn sie ihr Welken bereuen,
ist es an uns, ihre Reue zu sein.

Alles will schweben. Da gehn wir umher wie Beschwerer,
legen auf alles uns selbst, vom Gewichte entzückt;
O was sind wir den Dingen für zehrende Lehrer,
weil ihnen ewige Kindheit glückt.

Nähme sie einer ins innige Schlafen und schliefe
tief mit den Dingen – : O wie käme er leicht,
anders zum anderen Tag, aus der gemeinsamen Tiefe.

so the humble and self-effacing kneel
to tend the spring flowerbeds.
But they also cultivate – and conceal –
secret leanings towards every unsheathed blade

of grass, tender and green
and responsive to their caresses.
Ah, to be accepted, though the hot red roses'
reds simultaneously combust and threaten

to utterly overwhelm all
our hearts' understanding. For aren't we them?
Don't you long to succumb
to the green, the shy, all that's gentle?

LOOK AT THE FLOWERS

Look at the flowers, how loyal they are to the earthly,
through which we grant them their fate on the brink of fate –
and they know it. And if they regret their fragility
doesn't it fall to us to assume their regret?

Who doesn't long to soar? Yet we move as if weighed down,
sunk in ourselves, half-thrilled by our heaviness –
O how our example wears Things out, even
while they, like eternal children, rejoice.

If you were to fall into a profound sleep
and so slept with Things, how light-heartedly
you would wake to a different day from so deep

Oder er bliebe vielleicht; und sie blühten und priesen
ihn, den Bekehrten, der nun den Ihrigen gleicht,
allen den stillen Geschwistern im Winde der Wiesen.

Ô LACRIMOSA

(trilogie, zu einer künftigen Musik von Ernst Krenek)

1.

Oh Tränenvolle, die, verhaltner Himmel,
über der Landschaft ihres Schmerzes schwer wird.
Und wenn sie weint, so weht ein weicher Schauer
schräglichen Regens an des Herzens Sandschicht.

Oh Tränenschwere Waage aller Tränen!
Die sich nicht Himmel fühlte, da sie klar war,
und Himmel sein muß um der Wolken willen.

Wie wird es deutlich und wie nah, dein Schmerzland
unter des strengen Himmels Einheit. Wie ein
in seinem Liegen langsam waches Antlitz,
das waagrecht denkt, Welttiefe gegenüber.

2.

Nichts als ein Atemzug ist das Leere, und jenes
grüne Gefülltsein der schönen
Bäume: ein Atemzug!
Wir, die Angeatmeten noch,
heute noch Angeatmeten, zählen

a sharing. When they blossomed and praised
you, their new-found brother, you might choose to stay
in the companionable meadow, at peace, wind-grazed.

O LACRIMOSA

(trilogy for future music of Ernst Krenek)

1.

O tearful one, who like a sky restrained
grows heavier over the landscape of your sorrow;
when you cry, a drift of soft rain
slants over the sand-seams of your heart.

O weight of tears. Weigher of all tears!
Who felt you were not sky because you were clear –
and sky could only be a setting for clouds.

How distinct your land of pain, how near,
under the strong sky's wholeness. Like one
who lies there, his slowly waking face thinking
horizontally, into unparalleled depths.

2.

That emptiness is nothing but breath –
and that green consummation
of beautiful trees: a breath.
We, the still-breathed-on,
the still-breathed-on today, count

101

diese, der Erde, langsame Atmung,
deren Eile wir sind.

   3.

Aber die Winter! Oh diese heimliche
Einkehr der Erde. Da um die Toten
In dem reinen Rückfall der Säfte
Kühnheit sich sammelt,
künftiger Frühlinge Kühnheit.
Wo das Erdenken geschieht
unter der Starre; wo das von den großen
Sommern abgetragene Grün
wieder zum neuen
Einfall wird und zum Spiegel des Vorgefühls;
wo die Farbe der Blumen
jenes Verweilen unserer Augen vergißt.

SEI ALLEM ABSCHIED VORAN, ALS WÄRE ER HINTER

Sei allem Abschied voran, als wäre er hinter
dir, wie der Winter, der eben geht.
Denn unter Wintern ist einer so endlos Winter
daß, überwinternd, dein Herz überhaupt übersteht.

Sei immer tot in Eurydike – , singender steige,
preisender steige zurück in den reinen Bezug.
Hier, unter Schwindenden, sei, im Reiche der Neige,
sei ein klingendes Glas, das sich im Klang schon zerschlug.

this, the earth's slow breathing,
whose hurry we are.

    3.

But winter! Oh this secretive
turning-inward of the earth. Where around the dead,
in the sap's pure relapse,
courage re-groups –
the courage of future springs.
Where seed-hope is conceived
beneath rigidity. Where the worn-out greens
of endless summers renew themselves as ideas
in the mirror of anticipation.
Where the colours of the flowers
forget our eyes' slow appraisal.

BE AHEAD OF ALL PARTING

Be ahead of all parting, as if it were
already over, like the winter just passed.
For amongst our winters is one so utterly winter
that only by wintering through it will the heart last.

Die through Eurydice. As singer and praiser
constantly aspire to congruence, purity.
Here amongst the vanishing, in the realm of failure,
be the sounding glass that shatters as it sounds. Be,

Sei – und wisse zugleich des Nicht-Seins Bedingung,
den unendlichen Grund deiner innigen Schwingung,
daß du sie völlig vollziehst dieses einzige Mal.

Zu dem gebrauchten sowohl, wie zum dumpfen und stummen
Vorrat der vollen Natur, den unsäglichen Summen,
zähle dich jubelnd hinzu und vernichte die Zahl.

LE FOULARD ROUGE

Les hannetons ont fini leur ravage.
À ces rameaux déchus octroyés,
ils semblent pleins et innocents et sages
comme s'ils étaient les fils du noyer.

Et l'arbre même ne se plaint qu'à peine,
car dans son vide guérit tant de bleu.
La vie s'attaque à la vie sans haine.
Elle abonde dans les prés heureux

où les grillons s'exaltent cri par cri.
Tout au milieu des jeunes vignes bouge
la tête d'une fille au foulard rouge
comme un point offert à tous ces i

but also know the state of non-being,
the ceaseless groundswell of our inner vibration,
so that just this once you might brim with understanding.

Account for what has been – all the dumb, vacant
stock of teeming nature, her unsayable calculations.
Then jubilantly add yourself and close the account.

THE RED SCARF

The locusts' ravages are over.
Every disenfranchised bough
thinks them full and innocent and clever
as the walnut's sons. So much blue

heals in its voids
that even the tree doesn't moan – for
life attacks life without rancour.
It abounds in the happy fields

where crickets celebrate, cry by cry.
At the very centre of the young vines moves
a young girl's head in a red scarf,
like a dot offered to each i

These notes are intended to help the reader who wants to identify which of Rilke's collections each poem comes from, and in some cases to give some background, or clarification of a particular word or point.

Individual books in which the poems in this selection were collected during Rilke's lifetime are as follows.

Das Stunden-Buch: The Book of Hours (1905)
Das Buch der Bilder: The Book of Images (1902; 1906)
Neue Gedichte: New Poems (1907)
Der Neuen Gedichte Anderer Teil: New Poems, the second part (1908)
Requiem: Requiem (1909)
Sonette an Orpheus: Sonnets to Orpheus (1923)
Duineser Elegien: Duino Elegies (1923)

All were published by Insel Verlag, Frankfurt am Main.

Other poems, uncollected during Rilke's lifetime, are referred to as 'uncollected' in the notes, along with approximate dates of composition. The French poems are referred to as such, and their source-books given.

There are many translated versions of Rilke's work available – some are mentioned in the Author's Preface – and the most recent critical German edition is *Kommentierte Ausgabe* (4 volumes) edited by Manfred Engel et al (Frankfurt am Main: insel, 1996 and 2003).

p. 19 From the introductions to their respective translations of Rilke's work, McIntyre, C. E.: 1997 Rilke, Selected Poems, *University of California Press (first published 1940); and Oswald D.: 1992* Duino Elegies, Rainer Maria Rilke *Switzerland, Daimon Verlag.*

pp. 22-3 'Le Ruban' / 'The Ribbon': Poem 13 of 'Affectionate Taxes to France', from the *Complete French Poems of Rainer Maria Rilke*, translated by A. Poulin, Jr. The translator suggests the volume's title reflects the fact that Rilke lived in France for many years, but was never a taxpaying citizen. I gave the poem this title.

pp. 22-3 'Ich Liebe meines Wesens Dunkelstunden' / 'I love my nature's darkest hours': From the *Book of Hours*, Book 1, which is called 'The Book of Monastic Life'. An imagined monk speaks with God. 'Livres Heures' were mediaeval French devotional prayer books for lay people.

pp. 24-5 'Eingang' / 'Entrance': The first poem in *The Book of Images*.

pp. 24-5 'Früher Apollo' / 'Early Apollo': The first poem of Book 1 of *New Poems*.

pp. 26-7 'La Fontaine' / 'The Fountain': Poem 26 from the sequence 'Orchard', from the French Language Poems. Paul Valéry referred to "your astonishingly delicate French sound" after reading this sequence.

pp. 26-7 'Da stieg ein Baum. O reine Übersteigung!' / 'A tree rises – O pure transcendence!': First poem of Book 1 of the *Sonnets to Orpheus*, one of 59 sonnets written in two marathon sittings, while Rilke was also completing the *Duino Elegies*. (See note on 'The First Elegy'.)

pp. 28-9 'Die Gazelle' / 'Gazelle': *New Poems*, Book 1. One of a number of animal poems famously prompted by the sculptor Rodin, to whom Rilke was secretary for a while, advising Rilke to go and study – look at – animals in the zoo, and then write.

pp. 30-1 'Spanische Tänzerin' / 'Spanish Dancer' *New Poems*, Book 1.

pp. 30-1 'Geburt der Venus' / 'Birth of Venus': *New Poems*, Book 1. One of several longer, un-rhymed poems completing the book. Probably based on Botticelli's painting of the same name. The dramatic last four lines have been interpreted as representing the reality of womanhood, after birth even.

pp. 36-7 'Aufgesetzt auf den Bergen des Herzens' / 'Exposed on the Mountains of the Heart': 1914. Uncollected.

pp. 36-7 'Man muß sterben weil man sie kennt' / 'We must die because we know them': 1914. Uncollected.

pp. 38-9 'Dich, die ich kannte wie eine Blume' / 'But you, whom I knew as a flower': *Sonnets to Orpheus*, Book 1, number 25. Refers to Vera Knoop, a young girl whose dancing career was curtailed by illness. She turned to music, but died while still in her teens. Rilke found particular power and pathos in the fate of those who died young.

pp. 40-1 'Leichen-wäsche' / 'Washing the Corpse': *New Poems*, Book 2. The 'loom' of a lighthouse is light that can be seen from a distance at sea when the lighthouse itself is still below the horizon.

pp. 42-3 From 'Requiem für Eine Freundin' / 'Requiem for a Friend': 1909. The artist Paula Modersohn-Becker, a friend of Rilke's wife Clara – and whom he may have unsuccessfully courted before Clara – died in childbirth, while still a young woman. She had married the well-known artist, Otto Modersohn, and found herself both over-shadowed and confined to a domestic role. She broke free and went to Paris for a year by herself in order to focus on her art. Her husband and his family finally persuaded her to return, she became pregnant, but, tragically, her death followed. Rilke, who so vehemently held the view that marriage was incompatible with the artistic life that he could only manage a few months with Clara before they separated, overtly blames Paula's husband in this poem – he is the 'someone' who 'plucked her from her mirror'. Rilke's strong sense of death as part of life permeates this poem, of which these paragraphs are only a small part.

pp. 50-1 'Der Tod' / 'Death': 1915, uncollected. Rilke dreamt the strange image of the cup on the back of someone's hand. The last three lines refer to an actual, though unconnected, incident.

pp. 52-3 'Klage' / 'Lament': *Book of Images*, First book, part 2.

pp. 52-3 'Und fast ein Mädchen wars' / 'And it was a girl, almost': *Sonnets to Orpheus*, Book 1, sonnet 2. The girl is Vera Knoop. See note to 'Requiem' 1909.

pp. 54-5 'Orpheus. Eurydike. Hermes' / 'Orpheus. Eurydice. Hermes': *New Poems*, Book 1. Rilke's powerful and individual take on a perennial myth. Eurydice died as a result of a snakebite. The gods gave Orpheus, her grieving lover, the opportunity to go down into the underworld and take her back up into life. The only condition was that he should never look back while he was leading her out.

pp. 60-61 'Der Turm' / 'The Tower': *New Poems*, Book 1.

pp. 62-3 'Begegnung in der Kastanien-Allee' / 'Encounter in the Chestnut Avenue': *New Poems*, Book 2.

pp. 64-5 'O dieses ist das Tier, das es nicht giebt' / 'O this is the animal that cannot be': *Sonnets to Orpheus*, Book 2, sonnet 4.

pp. 66-7 'Du, Nimmergekommene' / 'You, never-arriving-one': 1913-1918, Uncollected poems.
   line 30 (p. 67) dwam: Scots for 'daze / day-dream'.

pp. 68-9 'Liebes Lied' / 'Love Song': *New Poems*, Book 1.

pp. 68-9 'Die Entführung' / 'The Abduction': *New Poems*, Book 2.

pp. 70-1 'Leda' / 'Leda': *New Poems*, Book 2. Compare with Yeats's 'Leda and the Swan', to which my translation refers.

pp. 72-3 'Abschied' / 'Parting': *New Poems*, Book 1.

pp. 72-3 'Die Genesende' / 'The Convalescent': *New Poems*,

Book 1.

pp. 74-5 'Christi Höllenfahrt' / 'Christ's Descent into Hell':
1913-1918 Uncollected poems. Typically robust Rilke
imagining of part of the Christ story. He grew to despise
Christianity and Christ in particular – for making guilt of
sexuality, interposing Christ between man and God, and
encouraging a sense of repressing life for later reward
rather than living it to the full now.

pp. 76-7 'Duineser Elegie: Die Erste Elegie' / 'Duino Elegies:
the First Elegy': 1912-1922. Rilke regarded the ten *Duino
Elegies* – long anticipated and struggled for – as his Great
Work. He wrote the first, and bits of others, at castle Duino
in 1912, and the whole scheme of them was already formed
in his mind at that time. However, he was unable to find the
place and concentrated effort required to complete them
till 1922, at Muzot in Switzerland. There they poured out
of him, along with the 59 *Sonnets to Orpheus* – which he ini-
tially thought lightweight compared to the Elegies – in less
than a month. They are a massive, concentrated summation
of his deeply felt and experienced inner longings moving
towards celebration and praise of life. Dense, and difficult
to absorb in places, they range over all his preoccupations
and idiosyncratic approaches to life, love, relationships and
death, many of which are also addressed in other poems
in this selection.

Line 46 (p.79) – 'Gaspara Stampa': Italian lady who
wrote 200 sonnets about her unhappy love for a Count.
Rilke believed the highest love to be that of women whose
love was rejected and who both mourned and upheld it
for the rest of their lives.

Line 93 (p. 81) – 'Linus' story': Linus, in myth, may have
been a son of Apollo who was a poet who died young. Anoth-
er myth suggests he invented music, and taught Orpheus.

pp. 82-3 'Am Rande der Nacht' / 'On the Verge of Night': *Book of Images*, First book, part 2.

pp. 82-3 'An die Musik' / 'To Music': 1918 Uncollected poems. Stephen Mitchell reports that this was written in the guest-book of Frau Hannah Wolff, after a concert at her house.

pp. 84-5 'Gong' / 'Gong': 1925, Uncollected poems. There are a couple of other Gong poems, including one in French.

pp. 86-7 'Ein Gott vermags' / 'A God can do it': *Sonnets to Orpheus*, Book 1, sonnet 3.

pp. 88-9 'Der Einsame' / 'The Solitary': *Book of Images*, First book, part 2.

pp. 88-9 'Du siehst, ich will viel' / 'You see, I want a lot': *Book of Hours*, the first book, the 'Book of Monastic Life'.

pp. 90-1 'Bildnis' / 'Portrait': *New Poems*, Book 2.

pp. 92-3 'Duineser Elegien: Die Vierte Elegie' / 'Duino Elegies: The Fourth Elegy': 1922 See note to Elegy 1.

pp. 96-7 'Irre im Garten' / 'The Asylum Garden': *New Poems*, Book 2. The asylum had previously been a monastery.

pp. 98-9 'Siehe die Blumen' / 'Look at the flowers': *Sonnets to Orpheus*, Book 2, Sonnet 14.

pp. 100-1 'Ô Lacrimosa' / 'O lacrimosa': 1925, Uncollected poems. Rilke wrote to the composer Ernst Krenek "you know that in general all attempts to enhance my verse with music have been unpleasant for me, since they are unrequested additions to something already complete in itself.... With the little trilogy 'O Lacrimosa', something remarkable happened to me; this poem arose for music."

pp. 102-3 'Sei allem Abschied voran' / 'Be ahead of all parting': *Sonnets to Orpheus*, Book 2, sonnet 3.

pp. 104-5 'Le Foulard Rouge' / 'The Red Scarf' from the *Valaisian Quatrains*, French language poems, 1922-26. Poem number 38. Valais is a Swiss canton in the Rhone valley, where Muzot, Rilke's last home, was situated. I gave the poem this title.

BIOGRAPHICAL NOTES

Rainer Maria Rilke was born into the German speaking elite of Prague in 1875, and died in Switzerland in 1926. He was witness to the great political and cultural revolutions in Europe in the first quarter of the twentieth century, and in the case of the radical new art emerging in Paris before the first world war was involved in reviewing exhibitions and writing articles about the new artists, as well as developing his own increasingly individual and virtuoso verse. He was secretary to the sculptor Rodin for two years, met Picasso and Tolstoy and many other giants of the artistic and intellectual community of the time, while also developing an increasingly devoted readership for his own work. He lived a semi-nomadic but genteel life, moving round Europe from hotel to borrowed rooms, from affair to aristocratic benefactor, always prioritising the promptings of his art over the demands of commitment to the conventions of bourgeois relationships. His awareness of his own calling as a poet, his immersing of himself in the role to the extent he did – as well as his controversial deliberations on love, sex, art and religious observation in both poetry and prose – resulted in a guru-like status and following in some quarters. The Russian poet Marina Tsvetaeva's remarked in a letter to him that he is "not a poet, but the very embodiment of poetry".

Today his reputation is equally as high. His *Duino Elegies*, completed in the same year as the *Waste Land* was published, are landmark expressions of the complexities of intellect and feeling a human life can experience. The *Sonnets to Orpheus*, written at the same time, read like exhalations after the great in-drawing of breath the *Elegies* demanded; delicate, thankful, ecstatic. The earlier two volumes of *New Poems* sound a new note in European poetry with their mix of sensual, observed scrutiny of Things, and their capturing of the inner essence of what is being observed. There are over four hundred poems written in French in the last years of his life, and hundreds more exploratory and far-reaching poems Rilke did not publish. Together with his volumes of letters, in which he himself said much of his creativity was expressed, and his extraordinary impressionistic novel *The Notebooks of Malte Laurids Brigge,* Rilke's poetry constitutes one of the great literary achievements of any century.

Ian Crockatt lives with his ceramic artist wife Wenna on a small croft in the North East of Scotland, close to gannet-crowded sea cliffs and under the flight-path of seasonally migrating geese. After many years employment as a social worker with children and families, he is working on a PhD thesis at Aberdeen University, focusing on the translation of Old Norse skaldic poetry.

He has published several collections of his own poetry, Including *Flood Alert* (Chapman Publications, 1996), *Original Myths* (Cruachan Publications, 1999), *The Crucifixion Bird* (Northwords Folios, 2002), *Blizzards of the Inner Eye* (Peterloo Press, 2003), *The Lyrical Beast* (Salix Publications, 2004), and *Skald – Viking poems* (Koo Press, Aberdeen, 2009, reprinted 2011). *Original Myths*, which includes etchings by the Scottish artist Paul Fleming, was short-listed for the Saltire Society's Scottish Book of the Year Award in 2000.

He has been a prize winner in a number of national literary competitions, and was awarded Writer's Bursaries by the Scottish Arts Council in 2004 and 2008.

He is currently preparing a collection of poems translated from the work of Rognvaldr Kali Kolsson, a twelfth-century Earl of Orkney, as well as working on a new collection of his own verse.

Also available in the series
ARC CLASSICS: NEW TRANSLATIONS OF
GREAT POETRY OF THE PAST
Series Editor: Jean Boase-Beier

FRANCO FORTINI
Poems
Translated from the Italian by
Michael Hamburger

MARCELIJUS MARTINAITIS
The Ballads of Kukutis
Translated from the Lithuanian by
Laima Vince

VLADIMIR MAYAKOVSKY
Pro Eto – That's What
Translated from the Russian by
Larisa Gureyeva & George Hyde and introduced by John Wakeman
Complete with 11 photomontages by Alexander Rodchenko,
reproduced in colour.

ED. PETER ORAM
The Page and The Fire
POEMS BY RUSSIAN POETS ON RUSSIAN POETS
Selected, translated from the Russian and introduced by
Peter Oram

SALVATORE QUASIMODO
The Night Fountain:
Selected Early Poems
Translated from the Italian by
Marco Sonzogni and Gerald Dawe

GEORG TRAKL
To the Silenced: Selected Poems
Translated from the German and introduced by
Will Stone

Further titles of poetry in translation are available in
'Arc Visible Poets', 'Arc Translations' and
'New Voices from Europe & Beyond' (anthologies)

www.arcpublications.co.uk